Massachusetts Sabbath School Society

On the Frontier

Or, Scenes in the West

Massachusetts Sabbath School Society

On the Frontier
Or, Scenes in the West

ISBN/EAN: 9783337144142

Printed in Europe, USA, Canada, Australia, Japan

Cover: Foto ©ninafisch / pixelio.de

More available books at **www.hansebooks.com**

ON THE FRONTIER,

OR

SCENES IN THE WEST.

*Written for the Massachusetts Sabbath School Society,
and approved by the Committee of Publication.*

BOSTON:
MASSACHUSETTS SABBATH SCHOOL SOCIETY,
DEPOSITORY, NO. 13 CORNHILL.

CONTENTS.

	PAGE.
ADVENTURE ON A WESTERN STEAMER,	7
DEATH ON THE PRAIRIE,	19
GOING FOR LUMBER,	41
LIGHT FOR THE PRAIRIE,	70
A RIDE TO A WESTERN WEDDING,	89
THE LITTLE MOUND IN THE WEST,	119
A WALK WITH A STRANGER,	122
A FRONTIER TRAGEDY,	147
FRONTIER WOMEN,	186
THE MIDNIGHT CALL,	221
THE WORLD-WANDERER,	232
THE PASTOR'S DREAM,	242
A SMILE, A GLANCE, A HYMN,	247
A LOST OPPORTUNITY,	254
"NOT IN VAIN,"	261
THE PRAYING BANKRUPT,	265
"A SOFT ANSWER,"	276
THAT PROMISE,	281
AFTER MANY DAYS,	285
MY COUSIN,	289
INCIDENT IN A DEPOT,	300
MY STEP-MOTHER,	305

ON THE FRONTIER.

ADVENTURE ON A WESTERN STEAMER.

I HAD been for some years in poor health, and, at length, became almost prostrated in body and mind. Physicians advised a change of climate, recommending the North-west as adapted to restore the tone of my physical system, and save my lungs from disease.

Having never visited the region designated, I wrote a letter of inquiry to a friend who had just returned from that part of the country. Among other things, in reply, he said, "Should you go West, beware of the Mississippi River desperadoes. In taking a steamer, appropriate a state-room to yourself; do not, on any consideration, share one with a stranger. Let the money you take with you be in gold, and what you do not at once need secure about your person, thus." Then followed an ingenious method of secreting it. At the close of his communication, the caution concerning the money and the state-room was repeated.

Now, it is all very well, doubtless, for the physician with a lucrative practice to advise his patient to take a long and expensive journey, and the well-to-do merchant, with characteristic foresight, to describe the best way of taking care of surplus funds; but how one whose income was "five hundred a year, and sass," as Peep at No. 5 has it, could make such directions useful, was a question.

Nevertheless, in one such case, at least, that problem was solved; I will not say *how*, without the permission of the generous friends who saved heart and brain that tug. So one pleasant autumn morning found me on my way to the El Dorado of broken-down dyspeptics and pining consumptives.

A ride of fourteen hundred miles from my sick room, and I was at Dubuque, weary, yet impatiently awaiting the steamer that was to take me to the rolling prairies and bracing air of Minnesota. I had seen "the lions," and had nothing to do but that most patience-trying of all vocations in this railroad era to wait — for a delaying conveyance. Hour after hour passed, and I had about given up expecting the boat, when the porter, touching his cap, said, "The steamer is coming, sir. Shall I take your baggage to the landing?"

What a swarming hive was that Mississippi steamer! What part of the world was not represented in that motley, jostling throng!

My first business was to secure a stateroom, for it was plain that all on board would not have beds that night. Just then my friend's advice recurred, and I resolved it should be followed.

"I would like a state-room entirely to myself," said I to the clerk. "Can I be accommodated?"

"Can't tell about *that!*" said he, crustily. Then, looking over his book, "Yes, here's *one* empty — *forty-nine;* and here's the key," handing a key to which was attached a strip of leather marked 49.

I was enough of an invalid to retire early, and, having disposed of my valise, turned to fasten the door, when, on inserting the key, I found that it would not fit the lock. Returning to the office, my very meek statement of the unpleasant fact did not add to the amiability of the clerk. *He* couldn't be responsible for every key on the boat; if the wrong one had been labeled forty-nine, it wasn't *his* fault. " All is," said he, " that's the only state-room, and that's the only key to it *I* know of!"

There was no redress. I could only go back to the state-room, barricade the door with such articles as were at hand, and make the best of it.

How welcome " nature's sweet restorer" to the sick and weary traveler, and how *unwelcome* to have its blissful spell disturbed, thought I, as strong-lunged voices banished my slumber. Looking from the little window at the head of my berth, an animated scene was presented. On an elevated stand was perched a well-dressed man, playing on a shrill-voiced accordeon a popular air, accompanying it with a superb voice; the swaying mass of humanity around joining in the chorus; scores of voices in unison making stentorian melody. I was in no mood to sympathize with their enjoyment, but felt rather like the old lady, who, not approving of martial music, as the military pageant was passing, stepped out, and requested the band to stop playing. Till eleven o'clock the noisy music continued, when a tall, red-faced man, who made it his business to tease the musician, dropped a satirical remark in one of the pauses in the concert about a certain duet by a cracked voice and a badly cracked accordeon. The leader of the orchestra, with the over-sensitiveness of his class, declared, in high wrath, he would play no more — an announcement which, very ungratefully, was received with cheers, and the passengers separated for the night.

Just from the sick room, the journey and the loss of rest had so jaded me, that at once, as soon as it was quiet, I fell into a deep sleep. Suddenly, however, I was again aroused, by the falling of some article to the floor, and, rising upon my elbow, saw a face peering in at the door, as if some one was making exertions to enter.

It was a swarthy face, with shaggy eyebrows and heavy black beard, and the reader can feel assured it did not impress me at all favorably in the dim light and the dead silence.

"What do you want?" I asked.

"I have come to turn in!" said my visitor, stepping fully into view.

"You have mistaken the number," said I: "this is my room."

"I think *you* are mistaken," he coolly replied: "this is forty-nine, I believe? Yes," added he, stepping back, and reading the number on the door, "*forty-nine*," then exhibiting a key on which that number was marked.

"There is something wrong," I replied, "and I can not submit to intrusion."

"And I can not be kept out of my berth," he rejoined, determinedly. "The clerk sent me here not three minutes ago, with this key, and here I intend to stay."

"We will see what the clerk says about it," said I, starting out to find him. My intruder followed; but the office lights were out, and save the echo of our footsteps, and the strain and rush of the boat, silence brooded in the vast floating palace.

"The clerk has turned in, I guess," said my new acquaintance, "the rascal! He was here not more than three minutes ago. What's to be done?"

I reflected a moment. A short time before, a passenger, walking the boat at night, mysteriously disappeared; his agonized family being put ashore the next morning penniless and without a protector. I must confess that, under the circumstances, I scarcely knew which to choose — the stateroom with the stranger, or the open boat without the stranger, but concluded to take the former. So, returning together, and taking the upper of the tier of berths, I resolved to keep watch for the rest of the night, ready for any emergency. My unwelcome companion took the berth next below me.

It was not hard to keep awake after the events of the evening; and yet the moments moved slowly. Full two hours passed, and I was deliberating whether or not to dismiss my suspicions and go to sleep, when weariness overcame me, and I dropped into a restless slumber. How long this continued I can not tell; but suddenly a hand glided across my chest, pausing at the very spot where the gold had been secreted. The feat was accomplished with surprising dexterity, and, glacing in the direction from which the hand came, I found myself gazing into the same eyes that had peered in at me from the half-opened door! But the expression! Never had I seen any thing so fiendish — such a look of murderous determination. The left hand was at the gold, while the right held a gleaming knife. I felt that my hour had come. And yet it was not the glittering blade that filled me with horror, so much as the pitiless, demoniac expression of those eyes glaring from out their deep sockets. The blood froze in my veins. All power of resistance or of motion was gone. I could even feel the keen point of the knife entering my quivering flesh, before, with one last, desperate effort, I succeeded in throwing off the death-like stupor. Happily, that final effort availed, and, raising myself in the attitude of resistance, I awoke — awoke to hear my new friend, who yet remained peaceably in bed, make our room resound with certain nasal sounds, which, if not as musical as one could wish, were not just then wholly unwelcome.

Morning dawned clear and beautiful, showing a more preposessing face on the person of my suspected room-mate. He was from the good city of Hartford, Conn., and, from motives similar to my own, had secured, as he supposed, a state-room to himself, and having *the key to the only empty state-room,* — "forty-nine," — was as much astonished at finding it occupied, as I was at being intruded upon.

"But," said he, laughing, "I had no objections to passing the night with you!"

"Why not?" I asked.

"Because I knew you to be an honest man!"

"Ah, how did you know that?"

"From your anxiety to be alone."

DEATH ON THE PRAIRIE.

The long, terribly cold winter was nearly over, when my hibernating was enlivened by a caller, — a man of some note with us, having traits which mark the frontier chieftain.

Brave, and physically powerful, he sometimes takes the law into his own hands, and settles quarrels. Not a few "new-country" differences, of threatening aspect, have vanished before his stalwart form. As when, for example, a tempting "claim" was in dispute, and the rival party had gathered in force to drive the other away. Coolly listening to the altercation, he would espouse the side he judged in the right, — perhaps the weaker; then, laying aside his coat, as their champion, offer to decide the case by an appeal to muscular force, announcing himself ready to meet "any three" of the trespassers. But, however, the challenge was not accepted. Whether the sight of that huge fist excited fear, or conscience, or both, it proved a potent pacificator.

He was also well read, — a fluent public speaker, when once under way, and in debate, an opponent not to be despised. A politician, too, he had graced more than one new State legislature. And though in his early days in Maine he stood well as a church-member, he was now, alas! an avowed skeptic; — perhaps not a strange sequence to years of migratory life in California and the West.

Many a fine chat had Mr. B. and I enjoyed together, seated before the ample clay-stick-and-stone fireplace in his cabin, as he solaced himself with his pipe of an evening; and though, at times, I pressed home the claims of religion, he was not offended, if not convinced. But this was before the fierce wintery blockade had cut off neighborly intercourse.

The object of his call was at once stated. It appeared that, recently, having got out of supplies, he had ventured to break a road to M——, a settlement eleven miles distant, to buy flour and other stores. While there, he heard that a lad, twelve years of age, was frozen to death on the prairie, the first of the season, and that the parents were so deeply afflicted that it was feared the mother's reason would be unsettled. His sympathies being stirred, he visited the sorrowing household to offer consolation. To his surprise, his words were powerless. Nothing he could say, however kind or well-reasoned, reached their case; and, baffled, he saw they needed divine sympathy, of which he could not speak. He advised them, therefore, to call in a Christian minister.

Weepingly, they rejoined that they knew not as there was one in all the region.

"There is one tarrying in my neighborhood," he replied, "and I doubt not he will cheerfully come, preach a funeral discourse at your house, and do all he can for your peace of mind.

"And now," said he, after narrating the above, "if you will set a time to go over, I will carry them word, that they may arrange for your coming, and give due notice of the sermon."

It was with no little satisfaction that I made the appointment. For what more exalted privilege than to bear the balm of the gospel to bleeding hearts! Moreover, the testimony my infidel friend had thus unwittingly borne to Christianity, was exceedingly gratifying, and led me to hope for his further enlightenment.

The day set for the services at M—— dawned calm and clear, with a slight relenting of the cold. A good brother had offered the use of his handsome span and a generous pair of "runners," and calling for Mr. B., who, with a show of reluctance, consented to accompany us, we set out. A choir had been extemporized for the occasion. It was composed of persons originally from various States and from Canada, a miniature specimen of western society. Strewing the bottom of the long pung with clean straw, and taking our seats thereon, the better to screen us from the sharp, frosty air, and carefully enveloped in blankets and buffalo robes, the ride was made quite comfortable.

"There's the house!" said Mr. B., at length, as we began to ascend a swell of land, on which stood a pretty painted cottage, reminding one of New England. On the extended ridge grew the burr oak, with almost the regularity of cultivation, — producing the illusion that we were passing through an eastern orchard. In the background were cleared fields, well fenced, and the river belted with forest trees. It was a charming place, and an exclamation of delight broke from our company. One glance assured us that this was the abode of taste and thrift. The interest awakened by exteriors was not lessened when I met the inmates. The master of the house impressed me as a large-hearted, industrious man in his business enterprises, and in social relations kind and affectionate. His wife and a married sister entered the room soon after our arrival, neatly dressed in mourning; the former pale and worn; the gentle, refined face of the latter, sad and sympathizing. They were from Vermont, accustomed to the best influences of that goodly State, the stamp of which was indelibly placed on them.

The story of the parent's sorrow was heart-touching.

Judson, the son they mourned, was the eldest of five children, — a child of promise; "the flower of the family," as the neighbors expressed it. He had a mind mature beyond his years, and was a dutiful son. For some weeks before his decease, a change had taken place in his health. Without any known cause, his bodily strength wasted.

And, on the subject of religion, his feelings became tender and earnest. That ripening for the Reaper, by unearthly culture, sometimes witnessed in children, despite the most unpropitious circumstances, just ere they pass away, was his blessed experience. Deep questions about God and Christ and Heaven he revolved by himself. Questions of duty he was often propounding to the parents' slumbering consciences. His father had been a consistent member of the church, and faithful in family duties years before, but in the absorbing cares of frontier life, and the destitution of religious privileges, becoming backslidden, he had forsaken the family altar, and his conversation was utterly worldly. The son, with shadows of eternity deepening on his pathway, and the Spirit gently leading him, became unhappy in view of the parental shortcomings.

With tearful, pleading eyes, he would often say, "Oh, why don't father read the Bible and have prayers as he used to, mother?"

And the mother would ponder these things in her heart.

One day an elk had been shot some three miles out on the prairie, and a party were going with a wagon to bring it in. Watson Freeman, a companion of Judson's, and two years his senior, was going with the hunters, and Judson asked his mother's permission to accompany him. Contrary to her custom, for she watched over her idol with jealous care, she gave her consent, "scarcely knowing," as she told me, "what she said." The boys, as the team went slowly, soon got out and followed on behind. Excited by the expedition, they noticed not that the horses were gradually leaving them, till a great weariness fell on the more delicate of the two. He complained of being too tired to walk, and his young friend called to the men: "Stop a moment and let Judson get in. He's tired!"

"Can't wait," replied the hunter; "if he wants to ride he must run and catch up!"

The poor boy tried to rouse himself to hasten, but in vain.

His companion, alarmed, entreated the driver to wait, saying, "Do stop, just a moment, Judson's so weak! Do let him get in; he can't run a step; he can scarcely walk!"

"Well, let him stay where he is, then!" was the rough answer. "If he's too much of a baby to walk he ought to have staid at home!" And quickly the wagon was out of sight.

Meanwhile the cold increased. The sky became overcast. And a snow-squall, such as frequently sweeps the prairies of the north-west in late autumn, set in. The blinding flakes were whirled about with the fury peculiar to the storm where the wind, unobstructed, gathers mightiest force, and the enfeebled boy felt a deathly chill striking to his vitals, and said, "O Watson, I'm freezing to death!"

His companion saw the danger, and, exposing himself to the terrible air, as he took off his own coat, and wrapped his friend in it, he replied, cheerfully, "There! that will keep you warm, I guess. Now take hold of my hand, and we'll go right home. I'll help you all I can. *I* can find the way!" And, turning about, they started for the settlement.

Those who have known, as I have, the hardy pioneer to become bewildered and lost close to his own dwelling, when overtaken by one of those violent tornado-like storms, his cries for help drowned in the roar of the tempest, will understand the nature of the task which that brave young heart proposed to itself.

An instance of the kind occurred about the time of the event I am relating. A settler, experienced in frontier life, had gone to attend to his cattle, which were yarded in a temporary rail enclosure, a few rods from his cabin. While busied there, suddenly the dusky wings of the snow-tempest obscured the heavens. Hastily finishing his task, he started for home. Already every object was hidden in the awful gloom, and how the maddened gusts charged upon, and smote and baffled him! — pelting him with the cruel sleet; filling eyes and nostrils, nay, almost burying him with the driving drifts. The sharp coldness cut to the bones. The whole air was in commotion, — hissing, howling, wailing, groaning. Downward rushed the heavy snow-clouds, upward shot opposing columns, with surprising speed and strength; from every quarter to every quarter the whirlwind hurled the swift moving flakes. He had cleared forests in Michigan, and conquered hardships in prairie-land, but now the strong man was at his wit's end; hoping each moment, as he was tossed about in the mighty tumult, to reach his destination, only to be perplexed in his disappointment. Meanwhile, the families at home — for two occupied the dwelling — had become alarmed for him. Two stout men set off for his rescue, shouting his name. They returned, unable to cope with the rage of the elements. Getting their guns, they made another attempt. The report of the firearms reached the lost man's ear. He had been whirled about near the locality from whence he had started; and when the sound of the gun reached him, in his bewilderment, he was going directly out *to the solitudes of the prairie.* A moment more and he would have been beyond recovery.

It was a mile and a half to the nearest dwelling, and they had gone only a few rods, when Watson perceived his playmate could proceed no further, and, with a heroism beyond his years, he took him on his back and bore him on, on; the raging winds disputing the way, and the snow beating against him pitilessly.

Three quarters of a mile — the neighbors afterward estimated — did that noble boy carry his precious burden, nerved to strange strength by the love that was in his heart, and the consciousness that life or death hung on the issue. But the hands about his neck relaxed their hold, and his own step faltered; so, coming to a lonely oak, he leaned his charge against it, and covering him up carefully with the over-garment, bidding him not to be afraid, fled for help.

As soon as possible, he returned with a wagon, accompanied by its owner and a neighbor. By the side of the tree they found him, covered with a fleecy robe, sitting there still and silent, a faint trembling of the pulse was all that told that life was not extinct. What had been his thoughts there alone amid the wild storm; what the tenacity with which his young heart clung to life,— the yearnings for father, mother, little brothers; what the agonized soul-cries that ascended above the voices of the tempest, piercing heaven, or what visions of angel ministrants strengthening him in the last conscious struggle, there was none to tell. He was speechless. Laying him gently in the vehicle, they drove for his home. Bursting open the door, they bore the child in, — rash, kind men! *Judson was dead!* Not an intimation had the parents received that evil had befallen their son, since a few short hours before he had gone forth in his young joy. The blow fell with stunning force, it was so sudden, so unexpected; and while the father was sorely stricken, the mother mourned in an agony that " refused to be comforted."

"Oh, that he had been taken away from before our eyes by disease, then we might have been prepared for it!" she exclaimed. "But to have him perish all alone, with no one near to speak to, no one by to soothe his last moments! Left, too, so brutally by neighbors who, if they had been at all hu mane, might have saved him from such a fate. And to bury him without a minister of the gospel to speak to us from God's word, and offer prayer, it was so revolting, so dreadful!"

" Did you have no funeral service?" I asked.

" Yes; but it was so different from what we needed, and from what we had been accustomed to. We were told that a settler, three miles from here, a smart capable man, was a preacher. And, although he was a Universalist, rather than have none of the offices appropriate to such an event, my husband invited him to officiate. He made some remarks, but did not pray, saying he was not used to praying. And so my boy was buried! We have never felt right about that funeral, and when I heard of you, I felt *so* glad! I have not heard a sermon for more than two years, yet I prize such privileges."

But silently the neighbors had assembled from miles around, some on foot, more in ox-teams. The rooms were crowded with an intelligent, strongly-marked audience, decorous and sympathizing. A deep hush was over all as I read those solemn, sweetly-consoling passages in the Bible that lead the thoughts from the perishable to the unchangeable, and reveal the life to come. How wondrously significant were they in that grief-shadowed, pioneer home! And how touching the oft-sung hymn, —

> "Thus fades the lovely, blooming flower,
> Frail, smiling solace of an hour!"

Never, however, had I read those fine words of Cowper with such effect: —

> "God moves in a mysterious way,
> His wonders to perform ;
> He plants his footsteps on the sea,
> And rides upon the storm."

And I felt impressed to say, alluding to the providential and gracious preparation of the lad for the sudden coming of the messenger, that, if the bereaved would seek grace to look away from secondary causes up to the great First Cause, confiding in his wisdom and love, I felt confident they would yet see proofs of a kind design in their affliction, and learn that by it God intended signal good to themselves and others ; a remark which subsequent events justified. But I will not anticipate.

The mother's sorrowful face haunted me all the way during the ride back. Few words were spoken by our little company, before so companionable. The gloom of the death-room was on us all. The very landscape seemed in unison with the scene we had left, as it stretched away to the horizon, smooth and treeless, wrapped in its fleecy shroud. As I glanced athwart the long, dull level, I thought of the races that once held possession here, now gone. What was that great solitude but a vast city of the dead, without a memento? Only one living thing appeared as far as the eye could reach. On a gently swelling mound near by, scarcely distinguishable, in its garb of pure white, from the snowy hillock, sat a large Arctic bird (*strix nyctea*). Naturalists say that nearly all the notes of birds are plaintive. With a moaning scream, like one in distress, the bird soared over us, his eagle size and swan-like plumage adding majesty to his lonely flight. The whole was in unison with the sad emotions that ruled our hearts.

"I thank you for calling for me," said my infidel friend, as he stepped out of the sleigh at his gate.

"And I thank *you*," I replied, "for opening the way for Christian labor on behalf of that afflicted family. If it benefits them, *you* brought it about. And my prayer is, that it may do us *all* good!"

"I hope it may," he rejoined, with a tremulous voice, as he entered his door.

The driver was not so much to blame as at first appeared. He did not realize that the boy was so feeble. Many kind-hearted people, blessed with health, cannot be made to understand the condition of those less favored in this regard. How often the incurably diseased, suffering indescribable horrors, subjected to the slow-wasting power of some chronic complaint, are contemptuously treated by those who might cheer their gloom and soften their hard lot. Ah! dear reader, let us never be wanting in tenderest sympathy toward the frail, sensitive invalid, soon perhaps to be hidden from our sight by the clinging turf.

GOING FOR LUMBER.

Autumn's breath was growing frosty, reminding us that Winter was on his way, and our house was still unfinished; the floors were yet to be laid, and the roof boarded and shingled. The neighbor who volunteered to "draw the minister's lumber," had taken long journeys with that object in view, but without accomplishing his purpose, for the mills could not supply the demand, so great had been the immigration. So I resolved to go for it myself.

But every thing available, biped and quadruped, was over-busy, and as I had no "team," a further delay seemed inevitable, when relief came from an unexpected quarter. A Norwegian — a semi-Americanized, good man, hearing of my situation, called to offer the use of his cattle. He had them with him, a yoke of young, sharp-horned brindles, trim and muscular, with bright, undaunted eyes.

Now, within the year, I had landed, an invalid, in Minnesota. Forbidden, by my physicians, to preach for at least two years, I had, after the first few weeks, farmed, carpentered, felled trees, split rails, quarried stone, practiced medicine, taught school, &c., besides performing usual Sabbath labor. Having resolved to "take things by the smooth handle," I had found no little happiness in my many-sided life, but the prospect of a long journey with oxen did not look attractive I confess.

"Why, my friend," said I to the Norwegian, "it is twenty-seven miles to the nearest mill! I haven't patience to go that distance with cattle, they are so slow."

"Mine are fast enough," he replied. "I will match them against the best horses about here. I always trot them when they haven't a heavy load. You'll find them nimble, I'll warrant!"

It was no time to be finical, and I asked, "When can I have them?"

"To-night," said he. "I will leave them here and walk home. It is only six miles!"

The wagon-body was weak, and he requested that I procure another. I obtained one at last; an unwieldy affair, so heavy that three of us found it something of a task to adjust it to the wheels — a veritable Pennsylvanian — long enough, as they of the Quaker State say, "to reach from one mud-hole to the next."

The next morning I had mounted to the board seat, with my long teamster's whip, when a gentle voice called from the door, —

"Bring the wagon back safely if you can!"

The musical little laugh that accompanied this sally had something of foreboding in it.

For a while the path lay across prairie solitudes, unrelieved, save by a lively divergence now and then by the cattle, made in the spirit of mischief. Often, too, a "prairie hen" would run on before the team, keeping a few feet ahead, then fly off, with a whirring sound, into the long grass.

Seven miles, and "Slough Creek" was reached — a willow-fringed, bridgeless stream. Alighting, I was calculating, by the aid of a long pole, the depth of water and mud, and the steepness of the banks, when I was forced to run for the wagon, and managed to jump in behind, just as it was going into the gulf, for the brindles had concluded to wait no longer. Down we went, with a plunge and a shock, and up the other side at a round trot, the freakish creatures keeping on, in spite of me, across a level meadow, through a bristling array of blackberry and other bushes, to a log house. There they stopped. I got out to turn them into the path again, but they ran round and round the cabin. In a few moments a woman came out, and comprehending my trouble, seized the whip, and laying the lash on with her brawny arm, soon brought the cattle into subjection. They suffered her to guide them into the road. She disappeared, as I thanked her in pantomime — for she was a Norwegian, as unable to speak my language as I hers, and the brindles would not act as interpreters, yet that they understood her perfectly, and my English somewhat, I could not doubt.

It was once more "smooth sailing," and as the beasts behaved for a time with exemplary steadiness, for want of something else to do I fell to reconsidering the figure I had just cut, and trying to comprehend the character and qualities of my horned steeds. What sagacity they showed in choice of opportunity when about to execute a wild prank! how ungovernable they became toward me, yet obedient to a woman's voice and hand! I at once recalled a humorous description I had read of pig-driving in Ireland. The writer says, wittily, there was in Ireland an old breed of swine, which is now nearly extinct, except in some remote parts of the country, where they are still useful in the hunting season, particularly

if dogs happen to be scarce. (He assures
John Bull, on the authority of Phil Purcel,
pig-driver, that this is a fact.) They were
a tall, loose species, with legs of an unusual
length, with no flesh, short ears, as if they
had been cropped for sedition, and with long
faces of a highly intellectual cast. They
were also of such activity that few grey-
hounds could clear a ditch or cross a field
with more agility. Their backs formed a
rainbow arch, capable of being contracted
or extended to an inconceivable degree ;
and their usual rate of travelling in droves
was at mail-coach speed, or six Irish miles
an hour, preceded by an outrider to clear
the way, whilst their rear was brought up by
another horseman, going at a three-quarter
gallop! In the middle of summer, when
all Nature reposed under the united influence of heat and dust, it was an interesting

sight to witness a drove of them sweeping past, like a whirlwind, in a cloud of their own raising; their sharp and lengthy outlines dimly visible through the shining haze, like a flock of antelopes crossing the deserts of the East. Their patriotism, also, as evinced in an attachment to the land of their birth and Irish habits, was scarcely more remarkable than their sagacity. There was not, the distinguished author assures us, an antiquarian among that learned and useful body, the Irish Academy, who could boast such an intimate knowledge of the Irish language, in all its shades of meaning and idiomatic beauty, as did this once flourishing class of animals. Not that they were confined to the Irish tongue, many of them understood English too; and it was said of those that belonged to a convent, the members of which, in their intercourse with each other, spoke only in Latin, that they were tolerable masters of that language, and refused to leave a potato field, or plot of cabbages, except when addressed in it. To the English tongue, however, they had a deep-rooted antipathy; whether proceeding from the national feeling, or the fact of its not being sufficiently guttural, is not affirmed; be this as it may, says the writer referred to, it must be admitted that they were excellent Irish scholars, and paid a surprising degree of deference and obedience to whatever was addressed to them in their own language. For a critical knowledge of their native tongue they were unrivalled by the most learned pigs or antiquarians of their day; none of either class possessing, at that period, such a knowledge of Irish manners, nor so keen a sagacity in tracing out Irish *roots.*

I was adjusting this description, hyperbole and all, to my case, substituting cattle for swine, and Norwegian for Irish, when my comparisons were brought to a pause. We had entered primitive forests, belting a river which flowed through loftily rounded bluffs. From the edge of the woods I could see that the road wound down among the trees by a long, yet rapid descent, often making a curve to avoid a stump, rock, or tree. So I took my place by the cattle, resting my whip across their faces, to check undue speed; but soon, with an impetuous charge, away they went, the axles frequently grazing the oaks, the heavy vehicle imparting dangerous momentum, till, dashing through the shallow stream, as they could not fly up the opposite bluff, I overtook them.

My attention was now called to a peculiarity in the road. We had ascended gradually, till we were crossing bare rock at a suspicious angle, and still the way grew steep. Thinking I must have missed the path, and that a track I saw a few moments before might be the true one, I stopped the cattle and hastened to examine it, with a frequent "whoa!" The result showed that we were on the right road. Returning, I found that the cattle, with a quick movement, had gained the apex of the hill, and there they stood, ranged along the verge of a precipice of at least one hundred and fifty feet! The slightest false movement might send them over. As carefully as possible, I turned them down to the road again, — and they were models of docility the while, — but the instant it was done, they wheeled about, throwing the vehicle completely over, and steamed toward home, leaving the wagon-body on the side of the rock, and further down the hind wheels; and recrossing the river, they sped up the other declivity, while I shouted most despairingly after them. By taking a bee line, however, I succeeded in coming out in front of them before they emerged upon the smooth prairie. Then, there was the righting of the front wheels, the attaching of the others, the guiding of the perverse animals up the bluff to the ponderous wagon-body. Where *should* I get help to replace it, in that lonely place, seldom trodden by human foot? I felt that this was an extremity, and for a moment could do nothing but pray. Then I looked up the winding path I had come, hoping to see some friendly face. None appeared. Meanwhile the cattle were restless. So, summoning all my energy, — the energy of desperation, — to my own wonder, I raised the huge wreck from its resting-place and adjusted it to the wheels, and in due time reached the mill village.

"Have you any lumber?" I asked of the mill owner.

"No; I let the last go this morning," he replied. "A man was here from L——, and said he must have some for his own house and some for his minister's. I let him have a few boards to keep him from suffering, though I needed them myself. Perhaps you are the minister from L——? Well, I thought likely. But I haven't a chip left. Which way did you come?"

"Across R—— River, through the woods."

"No wonder you've been cast away; it's a terrible road. Let me advise you to take the other route going back; it will be prairie mostly, and though further, will be easier."

"I shall do so. But what is that?" I asked, as my eyes rested on the end of a board protruding from a mass of timber.

"Well, that *does* look like a board," said the easy proprietor, "but it would be a job to get it out."

And he turned away, while I turned over the oak timber till I had obtained more of a supply than the neighbor that preceded me.

"Six miles to the Norwegian," said the mill man, as I was starting off. "You had better inquire the way of him, as the road is a blind one, and he knows all about it."

The afternoon was half gone, but I hoped to reach a settlement on R—— River, and spend the night there. But the chapter of accidents was not full. As I was ascending from the low village plot, the pins that held the bows in the yokes dropped out in concert, as if in memory of past joltings, letting the cattle free; of which casualty, they were not slow to take advantage, scampering off like wild buffaloes. In vain I used all the arts of which I was master, seeking to coax, surprise, or drive them into the bows again, which I bore with me for the purpose. If for a moment they stopped to graze, it was with one eye on me, ready to spring away at my approach. Help appeared, however, in the person of a map agent, just from New England, having left college, and come West for his health. He recognized me at a distance, and filled with compassion, hastened to the rescue as fast as his lame leg, made stiff by a rheumatic affection, would permit. The scene now became ludicrous in the extreme, and I laughed till the tears came, at my own plight and the figure my earnest friend cut, dragging his troublesome limb after him, as he tried to head the cattle. Farm bred, the crook of his arm and his intonations were rural, to perfection, but, as if aware of his infirmity, the wily brutes would wait his coming, and then, just in the nick of time, shake their heads and dart by.

More effective aid was rendered when an emigrant wagon appeared. Its inmates, scattering over the plain, proved too much for brindles, and they were captured, and the wooden pins that, with a borrowed axe, I had made meantime, were driven into the bows with an emphasis, that said, "Stay there!"

Twilight overtook me crossing a succession of sharply-defined ridges, black as Erebus, for the prairie fires had just swept over them. Wagon tracks diverged on either hand, and when darkness fell, — and it was "pitchy dark," — I soon lost my way, and there seemed before me the only alternative of passing the night where I was. The tent-like clouds lifted slightly, and stopping the team, I was considering what to do, when I saw something white moving along. It proved to be a man in shirt sleeves.

"Halloo!" I shouted, and he came nearer. "Can you tell me where the Norwegian lives?"

"An' it's about a mile an' a quarter, kaping the ravine to the second right hand road, thin kape to the lift apiece, an' ye'll come to it. But do ye know the way at all, at all?"

"Never was here before."

"Thin ye can niver find it, sure!"

"Not unless you will show me the way."

"Indade an' I can't! Fur yer see I'm in me shirt sleeves, an' I've been shakin' with the ager, an' the night air 'll bring it on agin. I wouldn't have exposed meself, but me cattle have strayed off."

"Oh, they will be found, no doubt!"

"But the neighbors up here have their turnips out, and they swear they'll shoot me cattle if they git at the turnips, an' as there's no fence they'll be sure an' do it, an' me oxen will be kilt intirely!"

"But, friend, you see how it is. I'm lost, and you can help me. My cattle are swift; it won't take long to drive to the Norwegian's, so don't leave me here!"

"An' sure it's not Pat O'Connor that'll do the likes o' that!" said he, touched by the urgency of my appeal. And springing to the seat, and applying the whip, the heavy team rumbled along over the roughnesses, now leaning to one side, now to the other, then ascending a rise of ground, then diving down the other side. Soon it stopped, and the driver jumped out, saying, cheerily, —

"Here's the place! Jist mind the cattle, an' I'll stip over and inquire the way for yer — it's bad gittin' to the house for strangers."

After a few moments he returned, saying, angrily, "Bad luck to 'em! The cabin is full of Norwegians, for they've had a raisin', an' they're all drunk as bastes, an' fightin' like Injuns, an' niver a word can I git out o' them. Sure, an' I don't know what I can do fur ye now. 'Twouldn't be safe for the likes o' ye to go with me, fur thim Irishmen are bad enough for any thing, an' it wouldn't do fur the drunken bastes in the house yonder to know ye're about. But good luck to ye, I must go."

Some months before, I had come across

an English family, living, I now thought, in that vicinity, and I asked, "Is there an Englishman living near here?"

"And is his cabin in a fine grove?"

"Yes."

"An' has he grass land on the south, an' jist before his door a dozen acres of 'breakin'' that's not finced?"

"That's the man."

"Faith, an' he lives only a mile and a half from here!"

"Can you drive me there?"

"Sure, an' I wouldn't do it for all the goold in Californy; for it's meself that isn't well, an' me cattle 'll be murthered before I can git back!"

"But," said I, strongly, "you *must* do it. I can't lie out on the prairie. I don't think your cattle will be any safer for leaving me here."

"Are you a minister?" he asked.

"Yes."

Instantly he was aboard again, and there was something of reverence in his tone, as he said, "I wouldn't go with ye fur money; but — but — I'll not lave ye now."

It was past ten o'clock when the grove-shaded cabin rose to view. My guide hurried to arouse the occupants while I "minded" the cattle.

"Hilloo there! wake up!" he shouted, as he thumped at the door. "An' ould acquaintince has lost his way, an' wants a shilter. Wake up, I say, and not be slapin' like heathin, when a frind is frazin' in the cowld!"

A door swung cautiously ajar; there was a hum of voices, and the Irishman returned, saying, —

"It's all right with ye, an' I'll bid ye

good-bye!" extending his hand. Then, as the well-earned guerdon touched the palm, "Sure an' ye don't think I came for pay!" and warm-hearted Erin disappeared as mine host came up. But like the Dutchman, who, after a scene of pathos over his lost "poy" restored, found that it was *not* his "poy," so this Englishman was not *my* Englishman. On explaining the mistake, however, he said, —

"Never mind, I shan't fret if you don't."

The dwelling proved to be one of those wretched loggeries that, happily, form an exception to the social habits of the region. The inmates were as uncultured as their shanty was rude. The one room contained five beds, one without a stead, while a dirty cooking-stove stood in the center. The floor was "truncheon," roughly hewed. A hole in the wall served for windows. Size should set off grace or goodness. The huge wife could scarcely lay claim to an excess of the latter. Then there was a grown-up daughter, whose chief accomplishment seemed to be the incessant using of the floor for a pocket handkerchief. Having dressed themselves, both dame and daughter sat down to ask questions, and pare potatoes for the next meal.

"Can you give me some water?" I asked.

A rusty dipper, filled with a dubious imitation of that beverage, was passed with this caution, "Look out for the wrigglers! I always blow before drinking!"

Having satisfied the appetite for news, the husband said, —

"Well, old woman, perhaps the stranger would like to go to bed!" At which mother and daughter began to disrobe, so I stepped out a while. On reëntering, I was little relieved to find they had retired, for their bed faced the one I was to share with the man, and with heads propped up against the wall, they eyed me with much interest. This was not at all molified, when the sire observed, —

"You can turn in as soon as you please;" while, from politeness, I suppose, he waited for me to retire first, keeping the candle burning on a trunk at the head of the bed. Hoping the gazers would weary of their mood, and he of his, that I might extinguish the candle, I went out again. But when I returned, landlord was still up, and the feminines not a bit sleepy, so, "doing as the Romans do," by an ingenious gymnastic feat, I was quickly hidden beneath the coverlids, while my new friend laid aside his garments at leisure, got slowly into bed, pulled up the covering, turned over, and blew out the light!

A silver ray streaming through the aperture in the logs opposite, woke me, and rising, I saw that it was the morning star peeping in at our repose.

"You are not going now!" exclaimed mine host, rubbing open his eyes.

"Yes, I make such slow progress I must be off in season!"

"Won't you stop and eat a mouthful first?"

"No, I thank you. But if you will yoke the cattle, and tell me about the road, I shall be much obliged."

The directions were not over clear, and the prairie did not lack in wagon-tracks, and, as might be expected, some miles were added to those really necessary in order to reach the settlement at which I was to tarry for business and refreshment. The stay here was much delayed. A debtor proposed to settle his long-standing account by letting me have a cow. The offer might not be made again.

"Is she near by?" I asked.

"O, yes; just down by the fence there. 'Twill take but a moment to find her."

The moment was full two hours ere she was secured, and attached to the team. Then an estimable lady teacher wished to ride over with me to L——, and there was further waiting for "big box, little box, band-box, and bundle." Mooly, picture of meekness that she was, when we were a couple of miles from her accustomed pasturage, slipped her rope, and rapidly retraced her steps. Her homesickness met with no indulgence, however, for she was chased down and led captive back, which she retaliated by causing us innumerable vexations, keeping one or the other of us humans watching her, lest her horns became entangled in the wheels, or to urge her on when she held back at the risk of her neck, when the locomotives from Norway had an attack of the capers. Despite every exertion, night fell while yet we were some miles from home, bringing with it, what is rarely seen in Minnesota, a dense fog, obscuring the stars, and hiding the surface of the country beneath its misty vail. An uninhabited tract of burr-oaks and hazel-bushes was yet to be passed. The dim and tortuous path was soon lost, and we were wildly beating about to strike it again. At length the wheels run smoothly.

"It is the road," said I; "our wanderings will soon be over!" But immediately thereafter the cattle stopped, and refused to proceed. Passing quickly to their side, how thankful I was for their obstinacy. They stood on the steep bank of the Iowa, facing the water. The flowing current revealed our course, however, and ere long we reached our destination.

My arrival was greeted with a merrier laugh than that which celebrated my departure. The sight, no doubt, was mirth-provoking as our procession passed before the door. Ragged and soiled, with a mammoth squash, which I had bought of my English friend, crowning the load, the cow tied behind the team; the lady teacher, who, unfortunately, had been obliged to walk most of the way, to attend to the manners of the turbulent cow, bringing up the rear; — the show, it appeared, was worth the trouble of standing, lamp in hand, to witness it.

As for the lumber, it did double duty; not only keeping the winds at bay, but in the gloomiest weather suggesting memories, which had a most enlivening influence on our household.

LIGHT FOR THE PRAIRIE.

ONE fine, spring morning, such as Minnesotians rejoice in, services had just commenced in our little sanctuary, when two strangers entered. One of them I soon recognized as Mr. L., whose son Judson had perished from cold on the prairie. Himself and friend, — a most exemplary Christian, as I afterward found, — having no preaching in their settlement, had walked eleven miles to attend our meeting. As they were returning at night, I accompanied them a short distance for religious conversation.

Their presence had a wider significance than I had supposed. Mr. L. said that the funeral services of his boy Judson had awakened a general wish for preaching; and hearing that I was not engaged, the settlers at L—— were anxious that I should locate with them.

"We want the gospel," he said, with Western frankness, "and we don't mean to *steal* it either!" Then followed considerations tending to show that the speaker, and those he represented, were in earnest. Visits to L—— convinced me that it was a promising field of effort, and I did not feel at liberty to "decline the call," though previously I had scarcely determined whether to remain West or not. Accepting the generous hospitality of Mr. L., I became an inmate of his household, until the arrival of my family from the east. The shadow of their great sorrow still rested on them, stimulating in me desire for their spiritual good.

One member of the family, especially, excited interest. They called her aunt Flora. She was over sixty, stout and robust; her plain, almost repulsive countenance, wearing ever a sullen, imbittered expression. A more hopeless, forbidding face one rarely sees. She had also this peculiarity. She uniformly absented herself from our devotions, and if in the room when the hour of prayer arrived, would immediately leave till the exercises were over. I supposed, for a time, that some labor called her away, and wondered that domestic arrangements were not such as to permit her to remain.

"I do not get acquainted with aunt Flora," I said to Mrs. L. one day.

"No, I suppose not," she answered.

"Is she a professor of religion?"

"No, indeed; she *hates* religion," was

the intense reply. "I do not think she has read a word in the Bible or attended church since she was a child. You have noticed she is never present at family prayers?"

"Yes; I thought perhaps some duty made her absence necessary."

"Oh, no, she will not stay. No one can induce her to; it has been often tried, but in vain."

"What a pity! And she looks so unhappy. We must pray and labor for her; perhaps God will soften her heart, and lead her to peace."

"You would not speak thus," was the decided rejoinder, "if you knew aunt Flora's history. I have no hope that she will ever be a different woman. She has for years been the bitterest enemy to the Bible and to Christians that I ever saw."

"But," I interposed, "how often were the vilest outcasts brought in under the Saviour's ministry!—the lowest, most abandoned, as well as the fiercest opposers. How the grace of Christ was magnified when he saved Zaccheus and Mary Magdalene; and met Saul of Tarsus, and made him a 'chosen vessel.'"

"Well, you can try," she replied; "but you will be disappointed. If you knew aunt Flora as I do, you would not attempt it."

Alas! how often the nearest relatives are least hopeful concerning the starving prodigal! How prone we are, from very abhorrence of sin, to walk in the steps of Simon the Pharisee!

My sympathy for the unhappy woman deepened as discouragements were presented, and no public duties were able to take my thoughts long from her. The labor I was engaged in was absorbing and rich in encouragement. It was so novel in many respects, so different from the stereotype customs of the East, that I could not but be interested; — a young town rising in the verge of civilization; prairies being farmed and fenced; immigration, with its ceaseless tramp, tramp; its unbroken line of white-topped wagons, bringing in additions from almost every quarter of the world, all eager for the treasure that perisheth. And this great flock, scattered abroad as sheep without a shepherd, must hear and accept the "great salvation," or be lost forever. The reflection was full of incentive.

Our congregation offered a singular scene. In garb, what variety! From the well-dressed merchant, just from the East, to the shoemaker in blue overalls and shirt sleeves. From the dashing belle, late from the metropolis, to the unadorned wife of the backwoodsman. In opinion, too, how diverse, — Baptists, Methodists, Congregationalists, Presbyterians, Dutch Reformed, Episcopalians, Adventists, Christians, Lutherans, Campbellites, Universalists, Spiritualists, Mormons, — many of them sturdy thinkers, with mind and body invigorated by hardships overcome, and a climate itself a tonic. Gray-haired sires were there, and infants in their mothers' arms. In those assemblages there was nothing sickly or effeminate; no one could look on those strongly-marked, thoughtful faces, without emotions of respect.

But the work went pleasingly forward, and again and again the congregation removed to more commodious quarters. And from grove, ravine, and prairie the settlers poured forth, thronging in our place of worship on the Sabbath. Then the Sunday school was organized, with officers and teachers from various States, and its large Bible classes; and though various errorists and sectarians were there, the Bible and Christian influence were elements sufficiently controlling. Often I felt awestruck at the power of the Word of truth in abashing error, when brought face to face with it.

I shall not soon forget our first session after organizing. We had then no hymn books, and were mutually strangers.

"I wish we might be able to sing at the opening of this school," said I, "but, it has been suggested, that, as we have no books, and have come from places so remote, we may not be able to unite in this exercise of praise to-day. I wish, however, to make an experiment. In New England, all are familiar with the hymn, commencing,

'There is a happy land.'

Now I want all who know this to join me."

Before I was half through the first line, most of the audience were singing; many, I doubt not, with a tearful memory of other days. The effect can not be described. Many a hallowed association was called up at that moment, to thrill the hearts of wanderers from earlier influences.

But what an hour was that when, after many struggles, the church was formed! The rain and the "bad going" did not keep the faithful few away. A venerated servant of Christ, living a "mile and a half off" on the prairie, seeking relief from the painful disease that had interrupted a useful pastorate, was punctually present, and, grasping my hand, said, "I did not know how I should get here; and when I came to the stream, and found there was no way to cross, I did not know for a moment, but I must turn back; it was hard to do it, however, and I just *waded through*, and here I am!"

Then later came the longed-for blessing. The rain of the Spirit descended, and in many a household was heard the inquiry, "What shall I do?" and the rejoicing of new-born souls.

Mr. and Mrs. L. were both members of our little church, and the family altar was no longer neglected. Aunt Flora, however, remained outside of the widening circles of salvation; she continued to absent herself from family devotions. But at length there was a change, imperceptible at first to most. Her voice was losing its harshness, her manner becoming more genial, and, though taciturn still, various little offices of kindness attested her growing interest. The " two " who, by agreement, were laying her case day and night before the Hearer of prayer took courage.

I embraced an opportunity to say to Mrs. L., " Do yourself and husband discharge your duty toward aunt Flora? Do you pray for and labor with her? If I mistake not, the Holy Spirit is leading her to thoughtfulness — to God."

" You do not *know* aunt Flora," she replied, with a look of surprise. " She will never change; I can not expect it! "

Oh, how prone God's people are to limit his grace.

On Sabbath days Mr. L., in his large-hearted way, loaded his long wagon with neighbors, and, in his zeal to get people to meeting, sometimes sent the ox-cart too. All the family, save aunt Flora, went. One Sunday morning, as we were setting out, she stood in the doorway, holding a babe left in her charge for the day. There was a tender, pensive expression on her face, and I said: "Good morning, aunt Flora. It makes us feel sad to leave you behind. God can bless you at home, however."

I had never ventured much on the subject so unpleasant to her, but the parting remark was well received. I detected symptoms of deep emotion as she turned away, and I said to Mrs. L., "It would not surprise me to learn that aunt Flora reads the Bible after we are gone." Still the same incredulity.

About sundown, a few weeks after this, a messenger called at our house — for we were then housekeeping, some two miles from Mr. L.'s, — stating that aunt Flora had been taken suddenly ill, and wished myself and wife to visit her immediately. We were speedily by her bedside; but what a happy place was that! Suffering intense physical anguish, her face was radiant with heavenly light, and, with shouts of joy, she was triumphing in the love of a faithful and almighty Saviour.

"O Jesus! Jesus! how lovely, how glorious! I am his, and he is mine!" she exclaimed.

"How is this?" I cried, seizing her hand. "Do you, indeed, love the Saviour?"

"Oh, yes," she replied; "he called after me; he sought me, and found me; and I will praise him forever."

"This is, indeed, joyful news But when did this change take place?"

"It was the Sabbath morning when you

all left me to go to meeting. After I entered the room, something seemed to tell me that I was soon to die, and that I must prepare for it. I did not know what to do, but took up the Bible, thinking perhaps God would show me the way. While reading the chapter to which I opened, it seemed as if a great light shone on the words, and I saw how kind and loving Jesus was; how he loved sinners like me, and how he would receive me if I would only come. I came to him; and, glory to his name! he did receive me, and I am so happy! Help me praise him, all of you!"

"What chapter was it, aunt Flora, that was so blessed to you?"

"I do not know," she replied. "It was in the New Testament. It was about the woman that broke the alabaster box of precious ointment on the Saviour's feet, and wiped them with the hair of her head. And after I am gone," she added, " I want you to preach my funeral sermon from that chapter. I do not know where it is, I have read the Bible so little; but you can find it."

" We hope that you will get well, and live to do much good yet."

" No, no; my time has come, I am sure of it; and I am going home. I'm going to Jesus."

Mr. and Mrs. L. stood by in joyful surprise at her change. In earnest words she exhorted them to faithfulness and diligence; then calling in members of the household still unrenewed, warned and entreated them to seek the Saviour; their tearful promises witnessing to the power of her appeals.

One thing perplexed me. During the fortnight that intervened till she " fell asleep," she would quote passages of Scripture from the Old and New Testaments with surprising accuracy, copiousness, and pertinency, expressing herself almost wholly in the language of inspiration.

I said to her, "How is it that you can thus quote from the Bible, when, for many years, you have not read or heard it read?" The answer should thrill the heart of every Christian parent and Sabbath school teacher.

"Oh," said she, with a happy smile, "those are passages that I heard my father read at family prayers when I was a little child!"

> "Let those who sow in sadness wait
> Till the fair harvest come;
> They shall confess their sheaves are great,
> And shout the blessings home."

"How I love you!" she exclaimed, on

one occasion; "you are my spiritual father; and you (turning to my wife) are my spiritual mother! But, oh! how much more I love Jesus. Now I long to be with him." And thus aunt Flora passed away, — smiling, shouting, triumphing, — a "more than conqueror!"

At sunset, one day, I had strolled down to the quiet nook, by the shaded lakelet selected as Mr. L.'s family burial ground. It was on his land, and in sight from the windows, as if they could not trust their treasures further off. Judson, an infant son, and aunt Flora, lay there side by side, under those three grassy mounds.

I thought of that first, sad visit to the stricken family; of the singular way it was brought about, through the suggestions of my infidel friend; of the death on the prairie, and how this event, to which the mother was so long unreconciled, led to my removal to L.; of the subsequent labor and blessing.

Returning to the house, conversation turned to that very theme. I reminded them of the remark at the funeral, that if they would cease looking at secondary causes, they would find that the Lord had gracious designs in his dealings with them. "Now," said I, "see what has resulted! you have the gospel here, a Sabbath school, a Christian church, a revival, and in your own circle, "the blessing that maketh rich;" you are both in the church; the family altar, over the desolation of which your son mourned, is restored, and aunt Flora is in heaven. Is it not true that

'God moves in a mysterious way
His wonders to perform'?"

"Yes," replied Mr. L., "it was hard

losing our boy. But it has brought great blessings to us. God has done right," adding, in a husky voice, —

> "Behind a frowning providence
> He hides a smiling face."

A RIDE TO A WESTERN WEDDING.

AMONG the checkered scenes of missionary life on the frontier, there are not many more pleasant than a genuine Western wedding. The heartiness, the bold dash, the generous hospitality of the thing, and often the novel phases of social life which it reveals, together, of course, with the *fee*, which is rarely small in proportion to the ability of the parties, make the event quite welcome to the toiling preacher.

One day, on answering a modest knock, there stood before our log-house door a young man, barefooted, coatless, with coarse, well-patched pants and rimless straw hat, his face beaming with a bashful happiness, which would at once have suggested his errand were it not for his garb, or rather, want of garb.

"Are you the minister?" he asked.

"Yes," I replied.

Then followed a pause.

"Is there any thing," said I, breaking the silence, "that I can do for you?"

"Yes. I came to see if you could come down to Mr. Dearborn's next Thursday, and marry a couple."

"Where does Mr. Dearborn live?"

"Seven miles below here, on the other side of the river. They want you at two o'clock, Thursday afternoon."

"I will endeavor to be there at that time," said I; "but who are the parties?"

"Oh," he replied, with a look which was

its own interpreter, "you will know when you get there."

After getting all the directions needful for finding the place, I was about closing the interview, but my caller lingered as if he had more to say; and, after evident embarrassment, asked what I "charged for marrying folks?"

"I generally leave that to the parties," said I.

Then ensued another pause, broken, at length, by his saying, in a depressed tone,—

"I have no money now; perhaps you wouldn't come down and marry us, and wait for your pay?"

"That I will," I replied. "And, Providence permitting, you will see me at precisely the hour named."

The cloud lifted from the sunburnt face,

and smilingly thanking me, he hurried away with a light step.

Seven miles in prairie land is a short distance; but not being in a mood to walk, I engaged a horse of a neighbor. Meanwhile, for the two intervening days, it rained, or rather poured incessantly, moderating to a gentle fall on Thursday. On calling for the horse, however, the owner was reluctant to let him go.

"Elder," said he (he was a Methodist), "are you used to managing horses?"

"Somewhat — why?"

"Because," he added, "my horse is a high-spirited fellow, and has a bad trick of throwing folks. Few can ride him without getting hurt. The fact is, I didn't sleep a wink last night, worrying about consenting to let you have him; and I don't feel right to let him go without speaking of it."

"How does he throw his riders?" I asked.

"By suddenly jumping to one side. He's powerful at jumping — beats all the horses I ever saw in *that* line," said he.

"I can look out for him!"

"He'll outwit you, elder; hope you won't try it."

But it was too late to go in search of another, and pleading urgent business and willingness to incur all risks, the formidable beast was led out — a powerful, intelligent, fiery animal, black as a raven.

What can be more inspiriting than a horseback jaunt across a rolling Northwest prairie. So, despite the cold and rain, and now and then a prodigious leap by Black Hawk, the ride was most exhilarating. It was two miles to the bridge. On arriving there, I found that the freshet had swept it away. Just in sight, however, in the margin of a fine grove, was a snug little cabin, and riding briskly there, the barking of dogs and my shouts brought the proprietor to the door, a bevy of flaxen-haired urchins at his heels, with eyes brimful of curiosity.

"Is there any way to cross the river?" I asked.

"Yes; on the bridge," he replied, curtly.

"The bridge is gone."

"Well, then there *isn't* any way."

"But is there no place on the stream shoal enough to be forded?"

The settler scratched his head comically, scanned me and my beast leisurely, and said, —

"Take the road to the left, and you will come to the old ford; how it will be in this flood, can't say. You can try it, though, if you like; nothing like trying, they say."

There was *need* of trying, I found, on reaching the spot. There rolled the river, deep and wide, with steep banks on either side. What was to be done? Go back and wait till the waters subsided? That was not *Western*. The genuine pioneer never thinks of giving up an enterprise. A short experience in the vicissitudes of frontier life wakes up a self-reliance and love of adventure, which make danger and difficulty to be courted rather than shunned, — indeed, they are every-day occurrences, adding piquancy to privation and hardship. And, as I looked down into the water of the river, there rose to view the image of that ragged, barefoot, coatless, moneyless bridegroom; and memory recalled certain facts which I had learned about his borrowing articles of apparel for himself and bride, and materials for a wedding supper. Now, to disappoint persons in their condition was hardly to be thought of. So, chirruping to my good steed, we made the plunge — and a deep plunge it was, for the animal above as well as the animal beneath — for the former went nearly to his neck. However, the horse soon rose to the surface, permitting his rider, by a happy exercise of unwonted agility, to strike the saddle *a la Turk*, which position I prudently kept till the opposite shore was gained. Clambering up the steep bank, my borrowed steed went at a break-neck pace the remaining five miles to our destination. It was a small, framed house, perched on a swell of land in the midst of a wide prairie, dotted with an occasional cabin. The dwelling was covered only with rough boards, between which the ever-restless winds came and went at will. Alighting at the gate, a gray-haired man — the bride's father, who was cutting wood in the little front yard — laid down his ax and came forward to take my horse. He had, as I afterwards learned, served in the Mexican war, and had still a soldierly bearing. Taking the bridle, he said, —

"You are the minister, I suppose. We had given you up, thinking you would not come in such a storm as this. But how did you cross the river? We heard the bridge was gone."

"Horseback," said I.

"Well," said the old soldier, his eye kindling, "*a minister that can do that can preach, I know!*"

I had fulfilled my engagement partly from sympathy and the pleasure of conquering obstacles; there was, beside, a sort of presentiment that urged me on ; nor did I in the end regret that I yielded to it.

The interior of the humble dwelling, and its occupants, I shall not soon forget. What taste and neatness under the most discouraging circumstances! What method and fertility of arrangement where all was plain, and rough, and scant! It is on the frontier, where the appliances of elegant housewifery are impossible, that woman's fertile resources of tact and skill most strikingly appear — often making the rude log-house and simple, home-made furniture wear an aspect of comfort and taste not unfrequently wanting in homes of luxury.

The household consisted of the father, — already introduced, — mother, three daughters, and the young man who had called for my services.

"Mother is not well, and would like to

see you a moment," remarked one of the young ladies, showing me into an adjoining room, where loving hands had spared no pains to fortify its pining inmate against exposure, and soothe the anguish of suffering.

A bed, with its snowy counterpane and tasteful curtains, stood in a corner of the apartment. On it reclined the dying mother, the emaciated frame and hectic cheek marking her a victim of consumption.

"I am so glad to see you," said she, extending her hand. "It is a long while since a minister of the gospel has entered our door; and yet I regret you have been put to so much trouble and exposure in coming. God will reward you! But I wish to speak with you about this marriage."

I learned from herself and husband that they were from New England, and in this and subsequent conversations gathered quite a connected account of their peculiar domestic and religious life.

Mr. Dearborn, like many other good men, at the period when, by prophetic interpretation, the time of the end of the world was proclaimed to be ascertained by Mr. Miller and others, became a convert to that theory. Not that he had ever examined for himself, or was competent to examine, the premises from which such a conclusion was drawn, for he knew nothing of chronology, history, sacred or profane, nor of the principles of Bible exegesis. Indeed, his stock of information was never very extensive, but the lectures *sounded* well, the mathematical calculations seemed to be figured up right, and the fervor and confidence with which all were challenged, on pain of the most fearful consequences, to accept the whole as truth, completely captivated his feelings. His sincerity and conscientiousness none doubted. All his worldly prospects and possessions were sacrificed on the altar of his new belief; the little church with which he had walked in fellowship, he left, "shaking off the dust of his feet against it," because the light he sought to shed on the benighted minds of pastor and flock was not received; his children were taken from school, all business matters settled; and he waited, without a doubt to cloud his mind, for the fulfillment of his expectations at the time appointed.

"Forty-three" glided by, however, as if no such man as William Miller had calculated the symbols of Daniel and John. But then the " Jewish forty"-three, it was announced, would justify the theory. That passed. The "tenth day of the seventh month," was soon discovered to be the true time. When that, too, slipped by, the poor man was in a chaos of prophetic and doctrinal speculation. Not that he thought any more highly of the cooler judgment of the brethren, whom he had denounced for their dullness and hardness of heart for not believing in the period set by his fallible guides, or that he had any less complacent idea of his own superior piety and biblical wisdom — not he. But then, in order to adjust the theory to the passing of the time, new opinions were constantly started ; gourds, which came up in a night to perish in a night, and all the old doctrines in which his faith had been nurtured, in the wild excitements of the hour were being overturned, till he had little in common with his previous theological faith. However, his ingenuity did not forsake him, and he settled down upon this device, that Mr. Miller's calculations were true; the end had come, but in a different way; the mistake had been in the *manner* of the event, and not in the time; the six thousand years, supposed to be allotted to our globe in its present state, had passed, and the great Sabbath of rest had come. In accordance with this belief, he now strictly rested from all labor, deeming it wrong to do any thing for the support of his family, or for the spiritual good of others, albeit he still had to eat, and his wife do the cooking, and wherever he went he was ready to argue for the truth's sake. In this state of idle, morbid, talkative " waiting," he embraced a thousand vagaries — among the least harmful of which was, perhaps, when he became a non-resistant.

With such a life, his little farm in Vermont soon melted away, and without money or business his family were in suffering circumstances. One day, while in this plight, as he was wandering aimlessly about, he chanced to stop before a recruiting office. While listening to the shrill notes of the fife and the roll of the drum, he "had an impression," to use his own language, that it was his duty to enlist. Now, impressions had been, during the recent excitements, like a divine law to him; for, supposing himself to be of a class specially favored of God with knowledge of the scriptures, and of the indwelling of the Holy Spirit, as was his custom, he did not stop to confer with flesh and blood, but put his name down on the roll. Quickly, however, he awoke to the incongruity of the step, — he, a peace man, a Second Adventist, one who believed that the kingdoms of this world were wholly of Satan, that it was contamination to have

any thing to do with human government,
and sinful even for a member of the "Fifth
Monarchy" to cast a vote under the
"Fourth,"— he, a soldier by his own volun-
tary action, and that too in a war against
Mexico, — a war too which Mr. Miller was
teaching to be the commencement of the
great battle of Armageddon! But there
was no retreat; and the first his anxious
family knew of his whereabouts he was on
his way to the field of strife. Without
seeming to realize his inconsistency, while
yet drawing pay as a soldier, he prayed that
God would keep him from actual blood-
shedding, and believed that his prayer
would be answered. His expectations were
realized. At the battle of Buena Vista,
when his regiment was ordered to charge,
the spirit of fight overcame all other considerations, and he rushed with the rest,

shouting to the conflict. But suddenly, remembering his principles and prayers, he paused, astounded at his own conduct. Just then an officer rode up from the front, holding in his hand a disabled gun. Seeing the hesitating private, he said, —

"Here, Dearborn, take this," handing him the injured weapon, "and let me have yours, and you may go back and help at the camp."

As his new sphere was congenial, he made himself eminently useful in dealing out their rations to the soldiers, and guarding them from surprise by the enemy. He had a quick eye and active temperament, and was constantly on the alert. The tent from which the food was dispensed was on a slight eminence, surmounted by a flag. Santa Anna's artillery, drawn by oxen, would move round the hill, getting the range, but just as the firing was to be done, the vigilant Yankee would give the word to the men, and they would vanish from harm's way. By this course he saved many valuable lives. From this service he was transferred to the hospital, and was so tender and efficient as a nurse, that he was continued in this vocation. His pay now was quite respectable; and when discharged at the end of the war, he went home with a nice little sum, conscious too of having been useful in the army. His non-combative sentiments had also been untouched, for he had not fired a gun at his country's foes during his absence.

He returned to tarry but a short time among the scenes of the past. Although still clinging to certain features of his prophetic dogmas, he was disposed so to plan for the future as to seek to invest his money in some permanently remunerative way. For this purpose he turned his thoughts towards the "great West." Besides, the changes, disappointments, and poverty-pinchings of the family, had seriously affected the health of the wife. Isolation from cherished religious privileges, the violent sundering of dear and sacred ties binding her to the people of God, while this was only in keeping with the husband's rougher, more controversial nature, her loving, sensitive spirit was well nigh crushed in the process. Mr. Dearborn was filled with concern when he folded the shadowy form of his wife to his heart. He deeply loved her, and, hoping that new scenes and a Western climate might save her from the destroyer, he emigrated at once, making one or two temporary locations, then selling out and going further into the unsettled woods.

It was while on their way out that the young man, to whom their daughter was now engaged, made their acquaintance, and joined his fortunes with theirs. It happened under circumstances of great trial to them, and his presence and aid were peculiarly acceptable, indeed, indispensable. With untiring zeal he devoted himself to their comfort, and whether on the long journey in the emigrant wagon, or in the toils incident to making a new home, he was like a son and brother.

What the father's feelings were as he saw the affection that was springing up between those two young hearts, it is easy to imagine. And when, one day, as they were putting up rail fence, the young man, after a deal of hemming and throat-clearing, asked for the willing hand of the girl, the father for a moment was dumb with astonishment, then exclaimed, " What! talk of marrying, when I have often shown you that time can last at most only a few weeks or months longer ! "

" I don't see why father must make every body go by his notions," said the daughter that evening, weeping the while.

" Annie ! " replied the mother, " if there ever was a good man in the world, your father is one."

" Yes, I know that, mother," returned the child, " but I'd like to know what there is wrong in getting married. George read to me this very day where the apostle says, ' Marriage is honorable in all.' "

" Yes, but, dear, your father says that that was not meant for these last days."

" Then why didn't Paul say so, mother ? "

" Well, dear, I don't see this matter just as your father does. But let us be patient, and not cross him, and if he is in the wrong, he is such a good man I have no doubt he will be set right by and by."

It must be confessed, however, that the prospect looked rather gloomy at times to the lover and his chosen. But, like Jacob, he would serve seven, or twice seven, if he might succeed at last. To this end labor, money, every thing was devoted, till at length the old man leaned on him, and could not do without him. Meanwhile, Time — that silent exploder of shallow theories — had set aside many favorite ones of this warrior-adventist, while the mother, true to the intuitive kindness and good sense of her sex, lost no opportunities of advancing, in her own gentle, admirable way, the claims of the persevering suitor, till finally consent was granted, and the wedding-day set, as we have seen.

"We came here," said the mother, "because of my health, hoping that the climate might do for me what medicine could not. I now see it was too late. But for my husband and George's sake, who have sacrificed so much on my account, I hope this last settlement may prove productive some day. They have secured a good tract of land, that must be valuable by and by; but we are 'land-poor' now all our money is gone. Another season, however, we hope our crops will bring us something more than the necessaries of life. George is like a child to me; and what is more, he is a Christian. Annie and he are tenderly attached, and despite our present poverty, I shall rejoice in knowing that they are united before I am called away."

But the few friends that had been invited had come in; the simple words that make two inseparably one, were uttered; and then, as the table was being laid, bride and bridegroom poured forth their joy in Christian song. Strangely touching was it here on the lone prairie to listen to wedded love thus expressed. Very happy were they, and comely too, in the freshness and vigor of their youth. And, as we gathered around the well-spread board, the sick mother, taking once more her place at the head of the table, her face beaming the peace she felt, there was a glow at my heart, such as I never experienced before as guest at a marriage feast.

Their happiness was peculiarly artless and childlike; and the hymns they sang, what strange interpreters of that happiness! There was only one hymn-book in the house, and that belonged to the father, and was devoted to the idea that molded his thoughts. But what cared they, if the sentiment was of unearthly things, — if it only helped them warble their bird-like joyfulness? With loving looks, and smiling faces, absorbed in thoughts of each other, they struck up, —

"The chariot! the chariot! its wheels roll in fire,
As the Lord cometh down in the pomp of his ire;
So, self-moving he rides on his pathway of cloud,
And the heavens with the burden of Godhead are bowed.

" The judgment! the judgment! the thrones are all set,
Where the white arrayed throngs, and the elders are met;
From the east, from the west, from the south, from the
        north,
All the vast generations of men are come forth!"

Then, more plaintively, they sang, —

"Son of God, thy people's shield;
    Must we still thine absence mourn?
Let thy promise be fulfilled;
    Thou hast said, I will return.

> "As a woman counts the days
> Till her absent lord she see, —
> Mourns and watches, weeps and prays,
> So thy church will weep for thee!"

As the father led my horse out for me to mount, he said, "We thank you for coming." Then, as I was gathering up the reins, "I suppose you have never noticed what the Bible says about the railroad cars being a sign of the times? Our ministers are dreadfully in the dark about the day we live in!"

"Ah! is it possible that the cars are predicted; what prophecy is that?"

"In Nahum, second chapter, third and fourth verses," he answered, taking out his well-thumbed pocket Bible, and proceeding to expound, with much inward comfort, as he read, —

"'*The chariots*,' that's the cars, '*shall be*

with flaming torches,' — that describes them as they appear at night; *'the chariots shall rage in the streets,'* — the tracks are laid right in the street; *'they shall jostle one against another in the broad ways,'* — how they strike together when they are about to stop, or to start again, being hitched one to the other; *'they shall seem like torches,'* — in the night; *'they shall run like the lightnings,'* — going at the rate of twenty or more miles an hour; *'he shall recount his worthies,'* — that means the conductor taking the tickets, and making sure that all have paid their fare; *'they shall stumble in their walk,'* — none who have rode in the cars have failed to see and experience how difficult it is to go about when the train is in motion. And this," he added, triumphantly, "is to be fulfilled, — when? *'In the day of his preparation,'* — that is, when God is preparing to judge the world."

"But are you sure," said I, "that the prophet meant to paint the steam-cars of our day?"

"Certainly; does'nt he say ——"

"How, then, does it happen that he announces that this prophecy relates to the city of Nineveh, which has been destroyed thousands of years? as in the first verse, he calls it 'The burden of Nineveh.' And how is it that these 'chariots,' or cars, as you term them, he describes as having wheels, and being drawn by horses, driven by the whip, as in the third chapter, second verse? 'The noise of a whip, and the noise of the rattling of wheels, and of the prancing horses, and of the jumping chariots.'"

He stood in silence a moment, then said, "I don't know. I haven't had any light on that yet."

"Well," said I, " when you get the light,

don't hide it under a bushel, but be sure and let the clergy have the benefit of it!" and consenting, at his request, to preach at his house in a fortnight, I rode on.

"Well, elder," said my Methodist friend, as I alighted at his door on my return, "not a limb broken, eh? But you had to swim the river! Guess you didn't get much of a fee though, did you?"

"Never better paid in my life,—what's my bill for Black Hawk?"

"Well, seeing you feel so *rich*, I think I shan't charge you any thing this time. All is, I'm glad you've got back safe and sound."

THE LITTLE MOUND IN THE WEST.

AFAR out West, a thousand miles,
  I own a spot of ground,
On which, last year, with trembling hands,
  I raised a little mound.

A robin, with her fledgeling brood,
  Was singing then hard by:
That robin, with her fledgeling brood,
  Was happier far than I.

The leaves have fallen on that mound,
  The snows have bound it fast,
And, howling through the trees o'erhead,
  Have gusts of winter passed.

But now the Winter's icy bands
  Are severed by the Spring,
And round that lonely mound again
  The robins come to sing.

How has the little tenant passed
　　The autumn there alone ? —
The long, cold, dismal winter nights
　　That since have come and gone.

He could not bear to leave me once,
　　Not even for a day;
He grieved and pined in loneliness
　　Whene'er I was away.

But now he lies untended there,
　　Nor murmurs from his bed;
And down in mold and darkness keeps
　　The watches of the dead.

We draped him for his final rest,
　　'Mid sobs, and tears, and sighs;
We combed his hair, and tenderly
　　We closed his precious eyes.

Do rose and violet keep their place
　　Through all these wasting hours?
And does his little moldering hand
　　Still clasp its withered flowers ?

With such endearing cares we sought
　　The cruel grave to cheat
Of half its horrors; even his toys
　　Were buried at his feet.

How vain the thought to placate Death
With cheerful funeral rite!
I have a funeral in my heart;
I bury him each night.

The grief each idle passer-by
Prejudged would soon depart,
Is gnawing deep and deeper still
Into my withered heart.

And in my agony, I turn
To that far spot of ground,
Where all my earthly hopes lie dead,
Within the little mound.

A WALK WITH A STRANGER.

A WESTERN REMINISCENCE.

I WAS waiting at —— Landing, on the Mississippi, for friends from the East. The spring floods were subsiding. The low, level land on the other side, with its rich vegetation exposed to the hot sun, sent up sickly vapors, and each day brought some new cases of ague and fever. Lofty bluffs, between which the town extended, shut away every breath of air. At times the heat seemed like a furnace. Nevertheless, the chills often drove me out to the sunny side of the hotel, where I would stand shivering in my overcoat.

One morning I stood warming myself as

usual. The street had few signs of life, save that scores of hogs ran about grunting their love of liberty, intent on plunder, which consisted mainly in running their sharp noses into bags of flour that stood in tempting array at the doors of the stores. The traders kept a long whip ready for the porkers, but "practice makes perfect," and the hogs would often outwit them.

An instance amused me. A shopkeeper, seeing the hogs coming, waited till they were within reach, then, springing out, he applied the lash, and they ran squealing away. He saw them approach his neighbor's flour. Assured that his own in the mean while was safe, he returned to his counter. Scarcely was he there, however, when a long-legged boar rushed back with the fleetness of a hound, and, by a dextrous blow of his tusk, tore a bag from bottom to top, emptying the contents on the ground. At once his companions rushed to the spot. The flour quickly disappeared, and, as I was laughing at the scene, a deep voice at my side said, "Wouldn't you like to take a walk, stranger?"

The speaker was a tall, powerfully built man, of about thirty. His sallow, sunken cheeks and wasted limbs, marked him a recent victim of fever. Nature had given him a manly, open countenance; but over it there rested a reckless, fierce expression. His abrupt address was not unpleasant to me; it was in keeping with Western frankness; but there was a something, illy defined in his looks, that made me suspect an evil design.

"I came down from St. Paul in the boat this morning," he continued, "and it's dull enough here. Up the river a mile or so there is a scythe-snath factory; I want to see it myself. You seem to be alone. What say you to going, too?"

It was a wild, lonely path, but I was in the mood for a change from the present monotony, and felt also a desire, after a moment's thought, to study my new acquaintance, and assented. My companion proved to be a person of varied information. He had evidently seen much of the world, and I became interested in him; yet could not help watching him suspiciously. Why did he leave the bar-room and select me as the companion of his walk? Why did he wish to walk at all,— he so feeble and weary-looking? And then there was an occasional glare of the eye, and it seemed to me a look of desperation. This mingling of the winning and the repulsive in the man kept my faculties observingly alert. Instinctively, however, I assumed a careless demeanor. He was not artful enough to be a villain by profession, and that was clear, yet, before the walk was half completed, I could not divest myself of a sense of personal danger.

"Come," said he, after inspecting the manufactory, "the bluffs shade the way, let's keep on up the river a piece?"

He was disappointed at my declining. On our return, he spoke often of the pleasures of foot journeys, and at length stated that he was to leave next morning for D——, a town some twenty miles distant; said he intended walking there, and pressed me to join him, as my course homeward lay in that direction. This, also, I declined.

That evening, as I was going out to a religious meeting, a second stranger accosted me,—"Are you a clergyman, sir?"

On receiving an affirmative answer, he said, "I hope you will pardon the liberty I take. I am Mr. N., of New York. I am here looking up land; have made some good investments, and wish to look around a little more. I have some money with me, and am really afraid of being robbed. You are the only guest at this house that has a room to himself. Would you not, as a great favor, permit me to share your room with you to-night? Last night I lodged with eight of the roughest customers I ever saw. I slept but little; but once I was startled from a doze, and looking up, saw a big whiskered fellow fumbling about my clothes. He protested it was by mistake, but I don't believe it; and," said he, his voice sinking to a whisper, "there's the very chap, as I live!" pointing to my morning acquaintance, who was just entering the bar-room. "A desperado, no doubt," he continued, much agitated.

On inquiring, I found Mr. N. was a wealthy merchant from New York — a speculator in land. The host at length reluctantly consented that Mr. N. should room with me.

The speculator, on entering my apartment, examined the lock to the door and added another fastening. He then seemed to breathe freely. His joy at the change was almost childish. Depositing his valuables at the foot of *my* bed, as if he thought somehow they would be safer there, he soon fell into a peaceful sleep, from which he awoke in the morning to renew his protestations of gratitude at what he deemed his escape from threatening peril.

"But," said I, "I am a stranger to you; how is it that you felt so safe with me?"

He replied, "I heard you asking for a meeting. I inferred that you were a religious man. From your appearance, I judged you to be a minister."

"But I meet many who sneer at Christians and Christian ministers."

"Sir!" he answered, with emphasis, "it's my business to FIND OUT WHO TO TRUST. Let infidels say what they will, the stoutest of them, if they had been in my place, would gladly have found refuge with a religious man."

Late in the forenoon, hearing loud voices in the bar-room, I glanced in. The altercation was between the landlord and the man with whom I had walked the morning previous.

"I will not pay so much. Give me back that dollar. It's every cent I've got. I was sick at St. Paul, and have spent every cent I had. I can't get work. I'm so weak nobody will hire me. Give me back the money, I say."

"I'll show you what I'll give you!" said the landlord, with a dreadful oath, "if you are not off mighty quick."

"But," said the other, in pleading tones, "I'm sick, I'm poor, I'm hungry — *hungry as a dog!* Have I eaten a crumb at your table? I've slept in your bed only one night, — last night I lay on the floor here, — that you know. And what am I to do if you take the last penny from me?"

The scene moved me deeply. It confirmed me in the opinion I had formed, that the stranger was in some extremity of trouble, and was not yet a villain. So I stepped into the bar-room. On seeing me, the landlord threw a quarter on the counter, and said, —

"There, take that, then, and be off!" The man took the silver, went out, and sat down on the tavern steps. An hour later, and he came to me, and said,—

"I am going to D—— now. Won't you go with me? I was going yesterday, but have waited for you."

Avoiding a direct reply, I started with him, and when the confines of the settlement were reached, while yet in sight of inhabitants, I turned, saying,—

"I must leave you now."

"What!" he exclaimed, fiercely; "you going back?"

"Certainly. Why should I go all the way to D—— afoot? Besides, I fear the fatigue of such a walk would be a poor preparation for preaching next Sabbath. His whole demeanor changed."

"Are you a preacher, then?" he ejaculated. " I thought you were a speculator!" and sinking down by the roadside, he looked the picture of wretchedness.

" Friend," said I, " you seem to be in trouble ; can I help you ? "

" Trouble ! " he replied, bitterly, " it's all trouble."

" I soon drew from him his story.

" I lived," said he, " in Western New York, and only two years ago thought myself perfectly happy. I had married to my mind. My wife loved me enough to connect herself with me against her parents' wishes — I being a mechanic, dependent on my own labor. They never were cordial to me, but kept themselves aloof, as if of another race. But she was always gentle, affectionate, and true. Ah, sir, she was indeed too good for me — too good for earth.

" My boyhood and youth had been industriously employed, and I had used such means of mental improvement as were within my reach ; but religion had always seemed a thing of gloom suited to the aged, or the last moments of life, but having no special claim on my attention. Never shall I forget the first evening after our marriage. Clara placed the Bible on the table, and said, —

"'Will you not read a chapter, dearest, and by prayer, seek God's blessing on our new life?' I knew not how to pray, but she did, and kneeling down, with sobs and tears, she besought God, oh, how fervently, to be with us in our journey together, and to enable us to live as he had commanded. She never faltered in her Christian course, never turned back, and was always happy. I looked upon her at times with feelings akin to awe. She influenced me more than any other being did before, and under that influence I was led to make a profession of religion, for I was powerless to resist her gentle persuasions. Still, I do not now think I ought to have taken that step; it was under the compulsion of a human love amounting almost to idolatry. Often I contrasted my hardened worldly nature with hers, and it seemed as if it could not be right that such a being should be united to one so unworthy of her.

"'Are you not an angel in disguise, come to save me from myself and from sin?' I asked one day; and I was sincere in the question, extravagant as it may sound to others. And when, after the labors of the day, as I approached our little cottage I saw her dressed in white, flitting among the flowers in the garden, or coming to meet me with a beautiful smile, the fancy would possess me that some visitant from a brighter world had taken compassion on my weaknesses, and in human form was seeking to lead me to the paths of peace and blessedness.

"After I had joined the church, she always encouraged me to keep up household worship. Were it not for her watchfulness and loving tact, however, often would the service have been omitted. Indeed, sir, it was her faith that I expressed, her desires that were breathed from my lips, I fear, for my heart was often cold and unbelieving, and my feet constantly inclined to stray."

"Did you have no enjoyment, no peace of mind, no real resolution to serve God in all this?" I asked.

"Sometimes it seemed to me that I did. But my life since shows that I was deceived. I loved her better than my heavenly Father, else why have I been tempest-tossed, at the mercy of circumstances, restless, complaining, wicked. Oh, if I had not lost her, I never should have fallen so low!" he exclaimed passionately.

"Then your wife was taken from you?"

"Yes; in a little more than a year she died, and an infant daughter was laid with her in the grave. Oh, the agony of those few last days of her life. I called in the best physicians of the region; they could neither save her, nor relieve her sufferings, while my heart was breaking with fear of the result, and anguish at her sufferings. But she, — why, sir, not a murmur escaped her lips; her peace grew wondrously, like the dawning of heaven, and while her body was racked with pain, her face shone like Stephen's before his murderers. Before her departure she was ever praying for me or praising God, for her soul was filled with heaven. Her last words were, as she pointed upward, 'We shall meet there, George.'

"When she died it was just before daylight one wild tempestuous night. I rushed frantically forth through the streets of the village into the woods beyond, and fell helplessly on the ground, overcome with the terrible emotions of rage, and grief, and wretchedness. I felt that life had now no charms for me, and that God was a hard being, a tyrant, who had remorselessly robbed me of all I loved. Unable to apply myself to work, what little I had got together for her sake was soon gone. At length I came West, hoping that new scenes might help me to forget the old. The change was favorable for a time. I found work, but fell sick. The few acquaintances I had were gone when I got about. I was in debt for board, medical attendance, and other necessary expenses, and have since been unsuccessfully wandering around seeking employment."

Briefly, misfortune had brought him to despair, and well nigh unsettled reason. Hard-hearted treatment had filled him with hatred to his kind. He had even been tempted to self-destruction, and later to commit robbery. His brain, as he expressed it, was "all in a whirl, and his heart hard as stone."

"Ah," said I, "you have been all wrong in your feelings — you have neglected one thing most needful for you in your circumstances."

"What is that?" he asked.

"It is that which your sainted wife found help in, — *prayer*. I also have seen sorrow, and have found it an unfailing refuge."

"Oh," said he, vehemently, "that I *could* pray!"

Commending to him the case of the publican and the thief on the cross, I added, "One anciently said, 'I am poor and needy, yet *the Lord* thinketh upon me!' If you seek him, he will be found of you, he will sustain you. And he will hear your cries, and open before you, I doubt not, a door of deliverance as it regards your temporal necessities. Will you not thus go to him and trust him?"

Then advising him to keep away from the miasma of the Mississippi and from the large towns, and seek a shelter till he was well among the kind-hearted prairie farmers, and placing in his hand something to help him on his way, we parted.

"That's a dangerous operation," said one,

passing, as some months after the incidents just narrated I chanced at a village fifty miles inland, and stood watching a group of men engaged in raising a "liberty pole." It was of great height, and no little enthusiasm attended its erection, for the place had just been made the county seat, after a spirited contest with rival aspirants for the honor. Being a stranger I could share little in the general joy, but was more concerned for the lives of those who pulled at the ropes by which the huge piece of timber was being elevated, than for the future of the town. Awkwardly enough, it seemed to me, was the raising managed by the gray haired leader of the enterprise, and as the pole swayed now this way, now that, I shuddered. But a sudden "hurrah" told that the feat was accomplished, and I was turning away relieved, when a man touched me, and said,—

"Excuse me, sir, but I believe we have met before."

It was my stranger acquaintance of the Landing. I had observed him, as among the most active in the raising; but in his new garb and new bearing did not recognize him. I had no time to reply to his greeting, ere he grasped my hand and said, tearfully,—

"I took your advice and have been prospered — been blessed;" and, pointing to a building just in sight, "there's my shop — I am a saved man!"

And, as we parted again, he said, "What a gulf I hung over when you rescued me! All the demons of the pit were dragging me to ruin! Thank God I was kept from crime — but how narrow the escape! and," he added, "I now think that my dear wife's prayers and labors for me have been blessed. I have a hope, for God did not wholly leave me. He saved me from the snare of the fowler, and set my feet in a large place. The furnace of affliction was seven times heated, but I am not consumed, and by and by I expect to meet her whom I love, and be with her forever, in the presence of the dear Saviour, who loved us and gave himself for us."

A coincidence connected with the facts just related is worthy of record. Our ride to the place was enlivened by a discussion between several of the passengers on the subject of benevolence. Some took the ground that it was the duty of every man to look out for number one.

"But," said another, "we are constituted mutually dependent; our Creator has made us stewards of each other's happiness, and when we assist an unfortunate neighbor we not only discharge a sacred obligation, but always receive in return a generous equivalent."

"In what way?" inquired his opponent.

"Oh, if in no other, in the satisfaction that flows from the performance of a deed of kindness."

"Not quite substantial enough for my use," returned the other. "When I invest money, I want money, or something equally tangible, in return. A consciousness of befriending somebody won't put meat into the kettle nor flour into the barrel."

"But what, after all," it was further urged, "is the motive of our money seeking? Is it not that we fancy that earthly possessions will make us happy? Certainly. But the experience of mankind shows that the soul can not be satisfied with perishable things. The millionnaire may be more wretched than the honest beggar by the wayside. The pleasure of doing good is, however, pure, ennobling, satisfying; a source of perennial enjoyment, purchased at a cost infinitely below its real value. Besides, our benefactions, bestowed without the expectation of any reward save that found in the pleasant thoughts and emotions which result, often come back to repay us in kind."

"Well, well," said the first, impatiently. "I prefer to invest where there is something positive to be realized. These uncertainties may do for those of a less practical turn of mind. I am a business man, and as such I want some security when my dollars are invested."

"Very well; the apostle says, 'He that giveth to the poor, lendeth to the Lord, and that which he hath given shall he pay to him again."

"I suppose," said the business man, "that you practise as you preach."

"Sometimes."

"Very well. When the funds you have disposed of in this way pay a dividend, let us know — that is all!" Our journey just then terminating, and not having proof at hand, the laugh rang against me.

On our return, after meeting the man of the Landing reminiscence, I said, —

"Gentlemen, you may remember our conversation on the subject of benevolence, and that I was requested when any money devoted to charitable purposes pays tangibly, to report. I have such a report to make at this time," — proceeding to repeat the story of my two interviews with the stranger, then showed the bank-bill that my grateful beneficiary forced into my hand. There was not a dry eye present.

"Well," said my mercantile friend, warmly, "you've got the case, and I frankly own that I envy you your happiness."

A FRONTIER TRAGEDY.

"Mr. Peterson, the Norwegian, wishes to see you," said the lady with whom I was boarding. "Something dreadful has happened, I know," she added, earnestly, "he looks so pale."

Going to the door, I was struck with the appearance of the caller. His cheeks blanched to a deathly hue, his eyes glancing apprehensively about, as he said, in a low voice, —

"You know Callahan, the one-armed Englishman, living near me?"

"Yes."

"He has disappeared; has been murdered, I fear."

"When did you first miss him?" I asked.

"Three days ago," he replied. "He lived alone in the cabin he was building on his claim — which joins mine. Being a single man, my wife had done his baking, for which he always came regularly. She had his bread ready for him last Wednesday, but he didn't come for it. Supposing some unusual business had detained him, she gave herself no uneasiness. But Thursday and Friday passed without bringing him, so she mentioned the circumstance to me. To-day I went over to see what the matter might be, but he was not there. Near his shanty, however, was a great deal of blood, and his hat and coat lying by."

"Did you make inquiries concerning him of the neighbors?"

"I did not dare to, but came away as

quickly as possible. I knew he had had trouble with old Ringe. Only last week, he said he was afraid the old man would put him out of the way, and I advised him not to stay alone on his claim. I have no doubt his fears have been realized, poor fellow! I scarcely dared leave home to tell you about it, for if old Ringe, or any of his tribe, suspected my errand, they would serve me in the same manner. Hadn't something ought to be done?"

"Yes. We must call the neighbors together, and search for the missing man."

"When shall we do so?" he asked. It is now nightfall, and to-morrow will be the Sabbath. Would it be right to attend to it then?"

"Certainly. Human life is sacred. And here, on the frontier, it is necessary to take prompt measures in such a case, or no person will be safe. We do not yet know that the Englishman is dead. Perhaps he is lingering in agony in some place to which, after being assaulted, he was borne for concealment. At any rate, this is, emphatically, 'a work of necessity' and 'mercy,' and steps must be taken at once to ascertain the facts, and if your suspicions are confirmed, secure the person or persons guilty of the deed."

Messengers were accordingly sent in different directions, inviting the settlers to start the next morning at nine o'clock for the scene of the tragedy, seven miles distant.

Some six months before the event I am relating, an aged clergyman who had immigrated to the vicinity, was obliged to go from home to buy hay. He invited me to accompany him. Crossing the open prairie, six miles, we came to a heavy growth of timber belting a sluggish creek. On the verge of the woods stood an unfinished cabin, before which were immense stacks of hay. The owner was a man of small stature, with curly black hair. As he mounted a stack, the winds that careered across the prairie blew off his hat, revealing a good brow and face. He had only one arm, with which he worked with a will, cutting off the hay and weighing it. His crippled condition excited our sympathy, and we helped him at his task, for which he thanked us with a manly gratitude. How strange to see him in the van of civilization, striving to do that with one hand for which many men found two insufficient. Yet he had made, and drawn, and put up that hay for sale (certainly no light proof of his energy and foresight), and for miles around his more able-bodied neighbors were coming daily to him to purchase. Besides this, he had quite a pile of rails split, ready for fencing. Falling into conversation with him, I learned that he was of Irish parentage, though born in England, and a Roman Catholic. He was candid and thoughtful, and on my friend mentioning that I was to preach at R—— River, next Lord's day, he promised to attend. He kept his word, showing much sensibility during service. At subsequent interviews, he expressed desire for religious instruction, and concern for himself as a sinner against God. His ingenuousness and deep feeling led me to hope for a happy result in store for him, and his lonely, disabled state — surrounded by strangers — heightened my desire for his temporal and spiritual prosperity. As on our first meeting, we stood talking together, an old man, withered yet sinewy and lithe, came and leaned against the rail enclosure that fenced in the hay. His complexion denoted a mingling of races. His wrinkled face wore that sinister impress that, when once seen, is not forgotten; hard, savage, insinuating, a mingling of the wild beast and serpent. I had not heard of him before; knew nothing of his antecedents, but shrunk from him instinctively, as, fixing his leering eye on me, he said, with an odious smile, that displayed in his almost toothless gums an upper and a lower fang on each side of a wolfish mouth, —

"Perhaps the gentleman is land-hunting. I've got a handsome piece of property up here," pointing to a cabin just in sight; "prairie and timber, that I will sell dog cheap."

Replying that I did not wish to buy, as

our team started, I said to my companion, with the "invincible assurance of a sudden presentiment," "that man can commit murder. How does that one-armed man dare to live by him?" Those two were "old Ringe" and Callahan.

The following Sabbath saw no small stir in our usually peaceful community. From various quarters men poured forth, afoot and in teams, many heavily armed, for old Ringe was the patriarch of a numerous and motley company, in which French, English, African, and Indian blood intermingled, producing, with their besotted habits, a degraded and desperate band. It was a balmy May morning. The air was fragrant with the scent of fresh grasses and spring blossoms, while the bluebird and the robin made joyous music. Could it be that amid such sights and sounds we were on our way to a scene of blood? On that holy, heaven-blessed morning, too?

"There's the cabin," said a voice at my side, arousing me from the revery into which I had fallen. The same dreamy quiet rested on it, as on the entire landscape. Not a person was to be seen as we drew near, and the birds sang as blithely from the covert of the woods, as out among the flowering hedges and shrubs of the green spreading prairie, away from "habitations of cruelty." On the side of the dwelling at which we stopped there was nothing to denote violence, but passing around it, a sight met the eye that sent a shudder through every spectator. In the hay that littered the ground was a deep sanguinary pool. Beneath the gory mass, the blood was still limpid; the quantity leaving no doubt on our minds as to the fatal character of the deed. A hoe leaned against the building, a pipe, with some partially burnt matches, near it; the dead man's cap and vest were not far off, while scattered around were bits of clotted paper that had been written over. These last I carefully gathered, placing them in a rifled pocket-book I had picked up. From the blood spot to the fence the grass was bent, and the soil disturbed as if the body had been dragged that way. On the rails were crimson stains, while over them, the trail could be traced towards the creek, which ran between us and a tangled grove. Old Ringe's window, forty rods north, overlooked our group, but not an inmate came to ascertain the cause of the gathering. It was proposed that I should take some of our number with me, and make inquiries there, while the rest hunted after the remains of Callahan. Two good men volunteering, we started on our mission. At the window, as we drew near, was the old man's son-in-law, Shuber, making ready to shave; at his elbow a mulatto woman watching us. Two barking curs disputed the passage as we approached the open door, at which Ringe's wife, also a mulatto, stout and ill-favored, her heavy features badly pitted by the smallpox, came to the door, and called out with a hoarse, savage voice, "Be still, I tell yer!" The dogs slunk away, while without another word the woman turned her back on us and reëntered. Heavy boxes were pulled roughly across the floor to serve instead of chairs for us, as we followed her in. One object, however, fixed our attention. Opposite the entrance, on a narrow bed, his legs pendent from its side, his back against the wall, sat the suspected murderer, as if fast asleep. His lower jaw had dropped down, his hands hung listlessly; no attempt at life-expression on his face to conceal its deformity. His aspect was haggard and revolting in the extreme. Purposely raising my voice to a high key, I said to the son-in-law, —

"Callahan is missing; we wish to know if you can tell us where he is?"

Continuing to strop his razor, he replied, jerking out his words, "Don't know where he is, if he isn't to home! Lives in the shanty down there. I ain't the feller's gardeen. Comes and goes jest when he's a mind ter; perhaps he's gone off a while. He'll turn up safe and sound, I warrant yer."

"When did you see him last, Mr. Shuber?"

"O, as to that, I haven't seen nothing of him since Wednesday morning."

"But haven't you thought it strange that he should be away so long?"

"Don't give ourselves, up here, any trouble about the *little Irishman*," the last two words pronounced with a hard sneer. "He takes care of himself, and we take care of ourselves."

"Well," said I, loudly, "perhaps your father can tell us something about him. Won't you ask him?" at which a slight flush tinged the cheeks of the sleeper, then quickly disappeared, while the son-in-law, continuing to ply the razor, replied curtly,—

"He's asleep."

Questioning other members of the household, who returned confused and contradictory answers, I again said to Shuber, "Perhaps Mr. Ringe can give us some information about Callahan."

"Father's asleep," interposed Shuber's

wife, "and we don't like to wake him up."

The old man's wife had been uneasily moving about, now going out of the house, now returning, avoiding conversation. Turning suddenly to her, I said, authoritatively, "We wish to ask your husband a question. You must at once wake him up."

Stepping to the bed, she placed her hand lightly on his knee, and ere she had uttered a word, he opened his eyes, stretched up his arms and yawned, saying, confusedly, —

"What — what — what do you want?"

"These gentlemen have called to ask about Callahan," said the wife, quickly. "They say he's gone off, or something."

"What, the little Irishman — as I call him? Some folks call him an Englishman, but I say he's an Irishman. O, he's all right. He's often taking a notion to go nobody knows where, and to come back nobody knows when. Can't put no dependence on him. But we never give ourselves any trouble about it; we're used to his tricks. Why, I don't suppose he knows any more about us, or we about him, than if he lived 'tóther side of the ocean. We don't hold to meddling with other folks' business. He'll turn up again, I'll warrant. Why, you *couldn't kill* the little feller if you should try."

"How long has he been away this time?"

"Can't say as to that. The last time we saw him was Tuesday afternoon. He was hoeing his potatoes there — right over there," pointing through the window; "and I said to the folks, guess the little Irishman means to get ahead of us. Soon after I saw him go toward his shanty, to rest, I suppose. You see he's got only one hand, and gets tired pretty easy, and then goes down by the cabin, and stands there and takes a smoke till he feels better. Well, as I was saying, he went down there, and pretty soon I heard a gun go off down that way, and Shuber says to me, ' What does that mean?' and says I, ' O, it's nothing but a wagon jouncing over a root or a stone in the road.' After that he was gone from the shanty, and I spoke to Shuber about it."

"When did you find out that he was gone?"

"Thursday morning. You see Shuber and I were at hunting deer along the creek, and we had to go right close to his house, for the creek is close by, you know. And says I, ' Wonder if the little Irishman's up yet? Let's give him a call, and see!' So

I called out 'Callahan, Callahan!' but he didn't answer. And we both hollered, but all was still as death. And, says I, 'The little feller sleeps sound this morning.'"

"Did you go back that way?"

"Yes, but 'twas on 'tother side of the house. And we called to him again, but he didn't say a word, nor show his head."

"When you went after deer, the path led you within a few feet of his dwelling and the fence. Did you see any thing unusual there? any blood on the rails, or on the ground, or any article of clothing?"

"No; it was so dark you couldn't see your hand before your face. Saw his vest, though, kicking about, that's all; but he's a mighty careless feller about leaving his things round."

"Well," said I, "you are a neighbor to him, and acquainted with these woods; we suspect something very serious has befallen him, and we want you and Shuber to go and help find out about it."

They consented; but as they walked, grew excited, and talked fast; and although no charges had been made against them, protested that *they* didn't murder " the little Irishman," that they knew nothing about the matter, that they believed he would turn up alive and well; — ending by stating that he was killed; that they knew who the murderer was; that it was a young German living in the vicinity, and that they could prove it.

" We think the body is in the creek," said a man in a low tone. " The trail ends there — we could follow it no further."

Stepping to where some willows had been felled into the stream, I was searching among them, when I caught sight of a pair of boots floating among the branches. They were fastened together with a rope. Taking hold of this to draw them out, to my surprise I found that they were on the remains of the Englishman. He was naked to the waist; his only hand was lashed to his feet; and as I deposited him on the bank, the blood still stood in what seemed to be deep gashes in the back. I had just stooped down to ascertain the character of the wounds, when, to our horror, old Ringe, officiously gathering a handful of dry leaves and grass, with a grim smile wiped away the blood, saying, —

"That's only where the blood has settled like."

He knew. The marks were indentations caused by the twigs on which the body had rested. Death was inflicted by a heavy charge of slugs shot into the back under the right shoulder.

Old Ringe sat over the ghastly form of Callahan like an ogre, gesticulating with the hand that held the clotted leaves, by turns asserting his innocence, and railing at the unconscious dead.

"*I've* nothing against the little Irishman. We had a little difference, it is true, but I jest taught him his manners, and he's been good enough since then. We haven't had a word together since last spring, when I slapped him, and he's been as quiet as a pig ever since."

His manner and language were horrible.

While waiting for the coroner, some of us went to a spring, a few rods distant, to allay our thirst. Old Ringe and his son-in-law followed, incessantly talking. He reiterated that he was guiltless, and implicated the young German. At length I abrubtly said,—

"Mr. Ringe, it is an old proverb that 'murder will out.' I have much faith in that saying, and for this reason: There is a God. His eye is ever on us. He has said, 'Thou shalt not kill.' He can alone give life. It is one of the greatest crimes possible for man wantonly to destroy that life. God is the Governor of the world, and he will punish the murderer. For the safety of society, and that bad men may be deterred from this highest form of sin, he takes special pains to bring to light the murderer. From him there can be no such thing as escape. Man is sometimes deceived and foiled, but God never!"

His countenance grew dark. The clamor of his tongue ceased, and for a few moments we were permitted to think in quiet as we stretched ourselves by the fountain's side.

Returning to the cabin, I had seated myself on a log, Ringe and Shuber by my side, — for they did not lose sight of me, — when the former stealthily left me, and went to the south side of the dwelling. A small ell had been attached to the main building. That only had been occupied by the owner, as the rest of the cabin was unfinished. In front of the ell was a high rail fence, making a snug enclosure a few feet square before the door. Ringe stopped at the little yard, and stood intently looking, now on the ground, now in at the door. Was he afraid that some clew had been left there by the assassin? His manner was eager and shy. Springing over the fence, I began to pick up fragments of letters thickly scattered among the loose straw, when suddenly it occurred to me that that was the place where the fiend had laid in wait for his victim. The Englishman had been shot on the other side of his house. From the condition of his field, and the fact that his hoe and pipe were near where he fell, it was plain that he had been hoeing, and had left his work in order to rest and smoke a while. The murderer having crept into his cabin, had no doubt shot him then. But if so, as there was no window on that side of the house, an aperture must have been made in the building, through which to take aim. A bed stood before the open door against the northern wall. Getting upon that, I saw an opening had indeed been made. It looked out over the bloody spot. Calling a neighbor, and directing him to stand by the spot, I found he was in exact range.

Ringe and Shuber were arrested on suspicion.

The justice, before whom the first trial was to occur, resided at a newly-settled town, twelve miles from our place. A friend, who acted as sheriff, invited me to ride over with him. Before the justice's cabin were a large number of persons watching our buggy as we drove up. Old Ringe and his friends were among them, and, as I alighted, he came forward, extending his hand as to an old acquaintance, saying, —

"Welcome! welcome! Glad to see the minister, — was afraid you wouldn't be here. *You* will want justice done. *You* won't stand by and see an innocent man like me falsely condemned. Look at my gray hairs and my dim eyes. Why, sir, these poor eyes couldn't *see* to shoot a man, even if I wished to take the life of a fellow-creature. But why should I do such a thing? I am almost in my grave, — have but a few days here, at most. No, no, you are a minister of Christ, and I know you can't have an old man like me hung,— I know you can't!"

This appeal, so unexpected, so affecting in its allusion to his advanced years, uttered in the thrilling tones of one who felt that his life was at stake, came near unmanning me. Releasing myself from his grasp, I said, aside to the sheriff, "How is this? Persons arrested for a capital offence at large — prisoners and witnesses mingling freely together! What does this mean? Why, they can agree on any testimony they choose!"

"Oh," replied the easy official, "never mind; the lawyers will pick the witnesses to pieces when they come to the stand!"

At the hotel a mile off, after tea, old Ringe met me again, with the most touching and insinuating appeals. They were hard to withstand, even from him. And when, next morning, he renewed his entreaties, I said, —

"Mr. Ringe, it is useless to appeal to me in this way. You know that I would not wrong you for the world. I shall state, as a witness, only what I have seen and heard, no more, no less. I can keep back nothing. I shall add nothing. This is all I could promise the dearest friend on earth."

As I spoke, a stern, bitter glance shot from his eyes, and a deathly pallor spread over his face. He avoided me from that time.

"Would you like to ride a few miles before court?" asked the sheriff. "I am going for two of Ringe's daughters, who were from home at the time of the murder. He says he can prove by them that the young German intended to kill Callahan. He states that they dropped corn for the German a short time before the murdered man was shot, and that he had tried to hire them to poison Callahan, that he might get his ' claim.' "

" Well," said I, " there is one request I wish to make; and that is, that the girls shall not be tampered with by the father, or any of his witnesses."

"Don't see the need of that. But if you wish it, I can take them to another house, and keep them there till you see the justice about it."

They were singular enough in appearance. Short, stout, tawny; with large, oval eyes; ears so long as to look inhuman; bold faces, and an oily speech. I had heard that they could lie and steal, and what might they not do, if their own father was ready to testify that their employer had sought to bribe them to poison his neighbor?

"Father didn't kill that man!" said one of them, sharply.

"How do you know that?" asked the officer.

"Because he's almost blind, he's so old. He couldn't see," she added, "if he was here in this wagon, to shoot the tail of that horse!"

"How does that agree with his deer-hunting before daylight?" said the sheriff.

The girls were kept secluded, despite the ravings of the father and the arts of his supporters; and it was significant that they were not summoned as witnesses, nor was the German accused.

During the trial, the State's attorney, taking me aside, said, "Search should be made through the neighborhood in which the murder was committed, for evidence that may serve as a clew to the murderer. I am persuaded that if any thing can yet be found, you can discover it. Would you be deputized for that purpose?"

"Yes, rather than let the criminal escape."

His horse and buggy were placed at my service, and, accompanied by a Frenchman, and a substantial farmer, I soon arrived at our place of destination. Cabin after cabin was visited, boxes and trunks opened, beds stripped, floors taken up, each nook and cranny scrutinized, without avail. Repairing to the creek, I noticed that on the stumps of the willows, that had been felled to conceal the body of the murdered man, gaps in the ax used, had left their impress on the wood. The farmer at once cut off the willow stumps, and taking them with us, we examined the axes in the neighborhood. In Ringe's house was one, the edge of which corresponded perfectly with the impression in the wood. The steel and the helve were also bloody.

"Now look sharp for bloody garments," said I.

A low, unlighted attic, to which access was had by a ladder, held the accumulated cast-offs of the household. Such a dusty, filthy collection! Only the friendship cherished for the inoffensive deceased, deepened by that peculiar interest felt in one for whom the Christian minister has toiled and prayed, and a strong desire that justice should be done, could have borne me through the repulsive task. The search was vain.

"Mr. D., hadn't we better give it up?" cried the farmer. "It's getting late, and we've seen all this house has to show!"

"A moment more," I replied, as I remembered that two beds, lying side by side on the floor, had not been removed. Lifting them up, we found beneath one a man's shirt, the arm and shoulder saturated with blood.

As we reëntered the court-room with the discoveries we had made, a deep silence prevailed. We had brought also another witness, who testified that old Ringe attempted, on one occasion, to burn Callahan to death; and that the old man had repeatedly said in his presence that he meant to kill him yet. The ax, willows, and garment were critically examined, the counsel for the prisoners not being able to explain away the evidence thus presented.

That night I slept in the same room with one of Ringe's lawyers. I shall not soon forget him, and the developments of our interview. He had a calm, keen eye; dark hair thrown back from a finely-turned forehead; a physiognomy sincere and refined. In his address there was a perfect air of good-breeding that inspired respect. He had an acute and logical mind, liberal acquirements, and a well-balanced intellectual and moral character. He realized my ideal of a learned, cultivated, upright lawyer. A *protegé* of Hon. Mr. Giddings, he had come to Minnesota on account of impaired health, and this was his first case in the territory. After retiring to our room, he wished to know the particulars of the terrible tragedy. The narrative impressed him deeply. I soon after fell asleep, but was in a short time awakened by his groaning and restlessness.

"Are you ill?" I asked.

"No," he replied; "but it is so horrible, so horrible. — that murder!"

Again, as he turned from side to side, he exclaimed, " Blood cries from the ground for vengeance ! "

And this was the man who, in the courtroom, was so unimpassioned, permitting nothing to pass that was adverse to his client, without the most searching scrutiny!

Before day broke, he said, " I have been dreadfully harassed by this case." Then, after a few moments, he added, " I have no doubt of the guilt of that old man. He's the murderer; but I can clear him. My partner has proposed a plan, which I am not at liberty to explain, that must be effectual. What shall I do ? Help spring the legal trap, and let the criminal loose, and thus succeed professionally, or not ? "

" Let me entreat you," said I, " to do right. God will bless you in it, and you will have a clear conscience."

"I will think it over," he replied, "and see what I can do," and he relapsed into his uneasy slumbers.

With eager scrutiny I studied his countenance in court the next day to ascertain his decision. In vain. I trembled for him, so severely loyal did he seem to his client's interests, and true to the pride of success. But his sterling, moral principle prevailed and Ringe and Shuber were recommitted.

He knew my anxiety, and said, as he passed from the court-room, with a happy smile upon his handsome face, —

"*Did I do right?*"

As for myself, procuring a box, I put the ax, willows, and shirt in it, in the presence of suitable witnesses, and committed the whole to the justice for safe keeping.

No jail had been built. The sheriff, therefore, took the accused to his own home. He lived quite a distance from the culprit's place, and it was not long before the cunning old man had so won upon his unsuspecting nature, as to be permitted to hire out as a day laborer. Wherever he went he pleaded his cause so effectually that the public mind became strongly excited in his behalf. He made also another diversion in his own favor. Among his children was one, familiarly called Bill, who was about eighteen years of age. He was the youngest of his boys, as well as the whitest. He was a great rogue, and was well known as such. His father called him half-witted, but he was an adept in villainy. Horse-stealing, robbing trunks, money-drawers, and stores of their goods, were among his exploits. Over the vices of his boy, Ringe whined and groaned among his new friends, and at last accused Bill of being the murderer. The lie was believed. When the witnesses of the State went to the second trial, they found that the settlers at the county-seat and vicinity had prejudged the case. A jury was drawn from the material at hand, and, although on hearing both sides most of them modified their views of the case, such was the previous condition of their minds, coupled with the fact, perhaps, as stated afterward by a juror, that several of their number were "opposed to capital punishment," Ringe and his confederate were cleared.

The terror that this result inspired among those who had been active in endeavoring to bring the perpetrators of the murder to light, can not be described.

The Norwegian went armed. Every night he and his family slept in the wretched attic of his low-roofed cabin, drawing the ladder up after them on retiring. But this state of things could not be endured. A party of resolute men went to the cabin of liberated desperadoes, and warned them off, on pain of forcible ejection. They soon disappeared.

The murdered man's valuable " claim," with its movable property, that his assassins had intended should become theirs, were sold at a good price. The fragments of paper which I had saved, on being put together, proved to be a letter from a brother of Callahan, residing in Lowell, Massachusetts, to whom we had the pleasure of sending the avails of the estate.

Who can predict the next new thing that will transpire on the frontier? One day, some two months after Ringe's final trial, an elderly man called on me, and said, —

" I have come to ask, sir, if you will not

make a five o'clock appointment, some Sabbath, to preach at my place. We have a very respectable community there, sir, now. Many new families have come in, and we would like to hear a gospel sermon now and then."

"Where do you live?" I inquired.

"At Slough Creek, seven miles from here."

Assenting to the request, the next Sabbath found me on my way there.

"Can you tell me where Mr. C. lives?" I asked of a well-dressed woman whom I overtook.

"Just through the woods, a few rods, the first house," she replied.

On arriving, what was my surprise to find that the meeting was to be at Ringe's log-house, now in new hands, and refitted and enlarged so as to present quite a neat and comfortable appearance. There was a good attendance and earnest attention. Among the audience, here and there, was one who had been partially of Ringe's company. They listened with no less respect because of the part I had taken in seeking to make the power of the law felt among the lawless dwellers upon our frontier.

FRONTIER WOMEN.

THE gentler traits of womanly character find little expression on the outskirts of civilization. When the wife and mother turns her back on her Eastern home, she enters on scenes which change the whole current of her existence, and often seem to make her a new being. It is interesting to notice how the transition process varies in different persons.

Some are *persuaded* into emigration. They start on the journey reluctantly, clinging to the old, familiar places. They have no day-dreams to lure them — no heart for the transplanting. From regard to others they join the restless tide that

sets toward the West. Others take the
"Western fever" as readily as their husbands, and clothe the stern realities of
removal with a roseate hue, seeing only
ease, comfort, competency in prospective.
But when, at the end of their journey, they
take up their abode in a wild prairie,

> "Alone, alone, all, all alone,
> Alone on a wide, wide sea"

of vegetation, and dead-level monotony;
no churches, no school-houses, scarcely a
neighbor to speak to, friends and kindred
far away,— how the thermometer of the
feelings goes down! how the air-castles
vanish!

But if you think either of these classes
make poor pioneers, you mistake.

There was Mrs. S., a practical, matter-of-fact person, unsusceptible to the love of adventure or of change. Submit any scheme to her, and, however dazzling it might be to an ardent nature, she looked at it in the light of fact, reckoning up the pros and cons with mathematical coolness. When, therefore, her husband became excited by accounts of the cheap lands, sure to rise, the fertile soil and healthful climate of Minnesota, she was calm. When he suggested emigrating, she was unmoved. Toil, deprivation, disappointment were invisible to his enthusiasm, but to her they stood revealed as verities, and to argue with her was useless. Indeed, looking at their present condition, why should she be in haste to abandon it for a life both new and dubious? Their pleasant home, with its broad acres and fine buildings, they owned. Educational privileges were excellent. Her husband was honored with office in church and state. But the more Mr. S. talked about a removal, the more his zeal was inflamed. The wife saw that his happiness was bound up in the matter, and more than that, his health, perhaps. Often prostrated by acute disease, he had been recommended to try the climate of the Northwest as a remedy. This consideration turned the scale in his favor. The homestead was sold, the furniture, farm implements, &c., advertised for sale at public auction. The avails of these, together with the "first payment" on the house, were to furnish the money for use in the new home.

Mr. S., however, after all his pleading, felt a little disheartened, when, the very night before the appointed sale, his goods took fire and burned up. But the wife had decided to go, and this untoward event did not discourage her. As they were to travel by their own conveyance, the emigrant wagon was made ready, and, with bedding, food, and cooking utensils packed, poultry-crate lashed behind, and the children aboard, they started on their *thousand miles'* journey! The first day all went "merry as a marriage bell," but at night, Mr. S. came down with ague and fever. He was utterly prostrated, and proposed to give up the expedition and return.

"No!" replied the wife, who had assumed the office of driver, "I am not going to drive these horses back again and be laughed at by the neighbors! Besides, if Minnesota will cure you, you need more than ever to go there now, and *I* shall not give up till we are there."

She kept her word; becoming coachman, doctress, nurse, cook, and guide.

She selected the camping-place at night, groomed the horses, took care not only of the babies, but of her husband. It was she that inquired the route, led the horses safely around "sloughs," and forded bridgeless streams, and, at last Mr. S. being still helpless, she picked out a "claim" on the frontier, and a valuable one it was, combining water, grass-land, plowing, timber, and nearness to a young town. She made their temporary shanty comfortable as possible, until, his payments coming in and his land rising, he was able to build a framed house. Not a word of complaint, reproach, or discouragement passed her lips through all this, nor did sickness and danger appall her.

An incident will illustrate her self-possession. There had been occasional depredations by the Indians. Still further on the frontier a bloody massacre of whites had taken place, and women were carried off captives. There were rumors of further trouble, as the savages were concentrating in force, and, mounted on their ponies, they could make a long sweep in a night.

One day alone, Mrs. S. stood before the looking-glass attending to her toilet. The cabin door was open, and her back toward it. Suddenly, she saw in the mirror the reflection of an Indian entering. Before she could turn herself, he had glided across the room in his soft moccasins, and laid hold of her. She gave no sign of terror, however — always the proper conduct in dealing with savages, as they respect courage, and suspect some hidden *power* behind it. He gently seized her long, flowing locks, remarkable for their luxuriant beauty, and measuring them with his arm, uttered an admiring exclamation, then released her, and departed as he came!

Mrs. N., another Western woman, was also quite a heroine. She was hostess of the first tavern at which the stage left me on arriving in Minnesota. It was a rough log-house. There was in process of building a small framed addition to it. Before this was a cellar, dug in anticipation of another "raising." Across this excavation we had to walk on a narrow plank to gain admittance to the house. The doctors I had left behind cautioned me not to sit or sleep in a current of air. That night, in company with a clerical friend, who felt quite merry at the aspect of things, I slept with the stars full in sight through the roof, while the winds sighed, and whistled, and moaned, and frolicked in and out the apartment, as the humor suited them. However, the next morning found us both, to our surprise, invigorated by the air baths we had taken.

At breakfast, I felt a little anxious to know how our merriment over hotel-life in Minnesota had been received by our landlady, who must have heard some of our criticisms. She impressed me as a lady of culture, and took our remarks as a matter of course. We soon learned something of her history. Her husband was from the East, a man of some property. He made his claim where I now found him, when there was scarcely a cabin in the region, confident that the site was a good one for a town. It was a wild, lonely spot, on the margin of a foaming stream, and between huge, shaggy bluffs, crowned with forests, in which the Indian and the wild beast roamed. Aside from the fish and game which abounded, all their supplies were brought from some trading point on the Mississippi. When her husband was on his long journeys for this purpose, she was sometimes left alone.

"Did you not feel discontented under such circumstances?" we asked.

"Not in the least. My husband thought it best to remove here, and that was enough. What was best for him, was best for me!"

"But were you not troubled by the Indians?"

"Yes, at that time, very much. They were afraid of our workmen, and would behave very well when a few white men were around, but they always endeavored to impose on us when unprotected."

"What did you do at such times?"

"Put on a bold face, and let them see that I did not fear them. I am astonished at the nerve I had. One day my husband was away. Quite suddenly a Sioux came into the house, and, without saying a word, took a seat. Another followed, and another, until a dozen had entered. Perceiving that I was alone, they commenced searching the house for plunder; examining boxes, trunks, and barrels. I had, however, by way of precaution, concealed what I could, and they did not find much. But they soon grew saucy and turbulent, and what added to my apprehension was, the fact that the leader of the party was half intoxicated. Still, as they had no arms, I thought I could manage them. After a time the chief chanced to see my husband's rifle, hanging overhead. It was loaded and capped. He started to get it. I divined his object, and started too, and as he was taking it down, I said, sternly,—

"Put that rifle back!"

He made a taunting gesture, and I attempted to wrest the rifle from him. We struggled,—I with the strength of desperation, for I well knew it would be a dangerous weapon in his hands, besides it was my only protection. None of his followers interfered while we contended for the mastery, but my courage led him to suspect that help was at hand, and, still grasping the gun, he asked,—

"White man coming back *bime-by?*"

A question which meant, Will he be long in coming? I quickly replied,—

"No. White man coming back bime-by *quick!*" This startled him, for he knew he had provoked retaliation, and hastily leaving, followed by his troop, they mounted their ponies, and drove off at full speed.

"I had also," said she, "a little adventure with the wolves. One day, feeling lonely, I spent the afternoon at a neighbor's. On my return at dusk, there had been a light fall of snow. When nearly home, I noticed that a large gray wolf was stealthily following me. I entered the door and closed it instantly; but, would you believe me, that creature, being very hungry, I suppose, sat watching on the door-step all that long winter's night! He fled next morning at the approach of a settler."

There was Mrs. L., too, a little butterfly of a woman, who had always been happy in New England. Her husband was a hard-working man, and took great pride

I NOTICED A GREY WOLF. Frontier, p. 198.

in beautifying the cottage he had built. It was not paid for, however, and at length he wearied somewhat of the toil needed to clear it of pecuniary encumbrance. Hearing of the cheap lands of the West did not lighten his burden, and he decided to emigrate. She joined in the project with alacrity, for her fancy painted a prairie home as a garden of delights. She reached their El Dorado under most forbidding circumstances. It was in late autumn, when the landscape stretched away bloomless and sear, and the cold rains were falling. It was indeed dismal without, and the cramped, uncouth log-and-mud house which received her as boarder, compared illy with the tasteful dwelling she had left behind. What a revulsion of feeling was hers! She wept for weeks, and refused to be comforted.

Some of the settlers thought her case hopeless — that she would never do for the West, mere New England doll that she was! But she had her cry out; and, like a true woman, when her husband, apparently moved by her grief, and homesick himself, — yet secretly glad of a pretext, — offered to give up and return, she resented it!

"Go back!" she exclaimed; "no, I shall not be ready to return until our Massachusetts friends see that we have been successful in coming out, and have been profited by the change." And of all busy women, Mrs. L. became one of the busiest. Henceforth it was smiles and work with her, and her quiet laugh and cheerful face made sunshine of darkest days.

Often her little figure might be seen

tugging her baby across the prairie to a neighbor's, to collect rare seeds, or bargain for hens. Her faculties were ever on the alert, devising something to make home comfortable; nor did snow, rain, loneliness, or sickness diminish her zeal. Neuralgia, aggravated by exposure, low diet and miasma, often prevails on the frontier. I have seen the hardiest pioneers writhe in agony, completely unmanned by it — never at such times venturing into the open air. Mrs. L. did not escape the disease. But what was my astonishment, on one of those doleful days in November, when a drizzling rain, driven by a cold wind, "sent mildew into the bones," to see Mrs. L. perched on the top of a load of lumber, drawn by oxen. Her face was bound up as if nursing the toothache, and she told me, with a ringing laugh, that she had ridden twenty-four miles at that snail's pace, and had had three teeth extracted!

Mrs. Myers, too, was another heroine whom I unexpectedly met, leading almost the life of a recluse in the deep gloom of a humble forest home. It was on this wise. Passing through the shaded path of heavy-timbered land, on K—— River, in a journey which I made on horseback, I came to the brink of a roaring torrent where stood a mill. As I was looking for a place to feed my horse, a man came forward, extended his hand, and said,—

"How do you do, Mr. D.? What brought you away up here? Don't you know me? My name is Myers, of P——, Massachusetts." But what a change a few months of another climate and new habits had wrought in my old friend. From the pale, almost effeminate dealer in dry goods, he had grown to be bushy-whiskered and portly, his cheeks fairly shaking with fat.

"Do you live here?" I asked.

"Yes; came here last fall, with my wife, and wintered among the bears and wolves, making shingles. You see," said he, alluding to his weighty appearance, "I have been a *gainer* by it. Never knew what it was to have an appetite before. The cold last winter made me ravenous; and though we had no market, you see we did not exactly starve. But, come, my wife will want to see you; the face of an old acquaintance will be next to going home again."

A low, snug shanty of oaken boards, just large enough to admit in its one room a bedstead, stove, table, and a few home-made chairs, was Mrs. Myers's empire — quite in contrast with her Eastern style. She was a gentle, lady-like person, had been a successful teacher before marriage, and was an accomplished musician. She cordially greeted me, saying, —

"I shall make no apologies. I am too glad to see a human being in these wilds, to care for aught else. Since we came here, not a person has been at our place, save the few who chanced here for shingles, all strangers to me, and such a long, cold winter I never experienced. Until the snow melted, late in the spring, we were quite alone."

"Were you not homesick and gloomy?"

"Only once, and that was the last of February. It had been an almost uninterrupted succession of storms. It was nothing but snow, snow, snow. We could not get out for any purpose, and our supplies were running low. We seemed to be completely shut away from the world — the only living creatures, save a neighbor in the cabin at the extremity of the woods, that we knew of, being a pack of wolves that sometimes swept by. On one occasion, my husband estimated that there were not less than thirty in the pack. That was a dismal time; and one stormy day, when the air was filled with snow, and the winds were sighing through the trees, my heart sank within me. And I rather suspect," said she, archly glancing at her husband, "that Mr. Myers did not feel much better than I did. Just then, when I felt like giving up entirely, I heard a little song — a clear, cheerful piping of a bird. You can not tell how it thrilled and cheered me. I looked from the window to see from whence the sound came, and there, right on the corner of our dwelling, sat the tiniest creature, caroling just as if it was June. This gave us both fresh courage. Said I to husband, —

"'If that wee bit of a thing can sing, much more can I!' and I struck up a hymn of praise to God, to which a certain bass voice made an excellent accompaniment. We felt better, and that's the last of the blues with us; though of course we had some hard rubs, and had to endure some things that in New England would have made us cowards. As, for instance, when our house fell down."

"Fell down! how did it happen?"

"You look astonished. I don't wonder at it. You see, when we came, husband could get nothing but green oak boards to build a temporary shelter with. And what with the shrinking, and the wrenching by the winds, and the snapping of the nails by the frost, one dark, stormy night, after we had been asleep some time, we were awakened by a strange noise. Looking about, how were we astonished to find that the boards had fallen apart, leaving us without protection! Hurriedly putting on our clothes, we had to scamper for the cabin I have spoken of for shelter till morning, when husband went to work and put this up, which has served us thus far."

Another case occurs to me.

On the south side of a little grove, at the very outpost of immigration, was Charles Wallace's log-house. He was from a thriving manufacturing town in Massachusetts. His business as a journeyman carriage-maker had enabled him to provide comfortably for his young family, and pay something annually toward the house in which they dwelt. It was true he had to work steadily and hard, and made what some would call slow progress toward competency; still the house was eligible property, neat, commodious, modern, and the little garden back of it yielded a bountiful supply of vegetables for the table. School, also, and religious privileges were all that could be wished.

Mr. Wallace was a thoughtful, reading man, of real worth and Christian principles, but very diffident. Men less well-informed, of sounder intellect, blest with self-esteem, and put-yourself-ahead-ativeness, would cut quite a figure in the eyes of an admiring public, while he, modest soul, was passed by unnoticed, unappreciated by the discriminating crowd. He had, however, a noble, generous heart, and glowing desires to be of use as a disciple of Him who went about doing good. These dispositions and aspirations, however, were repressed by his confirmed habits of self-distrust, and he was therefore often dissatisfied with his manner of life. He had read much of the spiritual destitutions of the great West, and came to think that if he could once be established where calls for laborers in the world's harvest were urgent, and laborers were few, that among new faces he could break the fetters of self-distrust, and do something for God and humanity. Moreover, one dull business season his employer failed, owing him quite a sum, which could not be collected. Now he turned his face towards the setting sun in good earnest. But the wife, how could he bear to tear her away from scenes so dear to her, and kindred more precious than life itself! He well knew the struggle it would cost her to leave New England, with its prized privileges, congenial society, and domestic comforts. She was one of those dear, loving creatures that love on, and love ever; the very trees, rocks, and rivers of her childhood and youth would cling to her affections with a deep grasp, and father, mother, brothers, sisters, how could she part from them for the distant and unknown West! He could scarcely hope for her consent to go, but had it cheerfully, whole-heartedly, yet with irrepressible tears and many forebodings, of which she did not speak.

Mr. Wallace had a clerical relative in Minnesota, who had influenced him in his decision to remove there; and that his family might go at once to some definite point, or home of their own, he wrote to the clergyman, commissioning him to purchase for him a farm. He did so. But on Mr. Wallace's arrival, it fell so far below his expectations that he sold it at a sacrifice, and went forth prospecting, locating at length where this account found them. It was late in the fall ere he could begin to build his cabin; the old settlers' story as to the mildness of the winters in that climate relieved his anxiety, however. The winter, nevertheless, set in early, and proved to be one of the coldest on record. He was overtaken without due preparation as to provisions. Nor was it otherwise with his neighbors, all new comers, like himself. The rigors of the prairie made it perilous to venture from home, and our emigrants, fresh from the abundance of the East, were brought to most wretched fare. Mr. W. was physically rugged, knowing nothing of the horrors of dyspepsia; and if there was only a sufficiency for the table, it mattered not to him what it was. Not so, unfortunately, with the invalid wife. There was little, at best, that she could eat that suited her diseased condition, and those very articles it was impossible to procure. One who was, providentially, an inmate of the household through the terrors and deprivations of that winter, says, —

"I had read of the rigors of the frozen North, and here I had a taste of them. For months, in the most sheltered nooks, and on the sunniest roof-sides, the snow gave no signs of thawing, while from morn till night, on the frosty atmosphere, luminous pillars, and circles, and mock suns witnessed to the intensity of the cold; and the nights, — O, *such* nights! why, you could *hear* it freezing, freezing; the swine in their pens piled and crowded together, quarreling for the warmest place, uttering incessantly cries of distress, with which mingled the sharp reports, like the discharge of pistols, of the oaken shingles on the roof, as the nails that secured them burst. I don't know how we got through that winter. Mrs. W. had courage, endurance, was free-hearted to a fault, but the commonest articles had to be dispensed with. The mills were so remote that the corn stored in the attic could not be turned into meal, greatly as it was needed, save by the slow and imperfect process of grinding in a coffee-mill, suspended against the wall. Mr. W. was anxious and low-spirited enough, poor fellow, frequently bursting out into bitter reflections on himself for bringing his wife to such a place.

And, indeed, how she was kept alive was a miracle; certainly she ate nothing, or next to nothing. Then, however, did woman's marvelous self-forgetfulness and fortitude shine out. Not a word of discontent or of depression ever escaped her lips. She was uniformly peaceful and hopeful, at least in the presence of the household, and her mild, sweet voice was often employed in singing some hymn of holy trust and cheer. I was ever admiring her spirit and wondering at her conduct. Yet that she was keenly alive to the situation of affairs, and that she suffered the pangs of unsatisfied hunger,— not having diet suited to her needs,— we were obliged to think. An incident impressed me deeply.

"Once, after retiring to rest, I awoke while yet it was dark, and overheard, in the apartment adjoining mine a low, suppressed whispering. It was Mrs. W. wrestling in prayer for strength according to her day. She had taken that hour to seek 'Him who giveth power to the faint,' that none but God might hear. Night after night did she thus pour out her soul in agonized supplication, yet on her face not a shade of anxiety could be discerned through the day.

"Often did Mr. Wallace, during the trials of that winter, and afterwards, resolve to return to Massachusetts.

"'Not yet, Charles,' she would say, 'not yet, till you have made enough to pay you for coming.'

"And repressing her own earnest yearnings for the faces of loved ones far away, by her gentle firmness she held him to his enterprise, till after some years, a good opportunity occurring to sell out at a fair advance, for his own sake as well as hers, he embraced it, and joyfully they retraced their course to the scenes they had left behind.

"It may not be amiss to add, at the risk of a digression, that Mr. W. was enabled, while dwelling on the prairie, to carry out his plans for being active in the service of Christ. And so did he win the hearts of others by his consistent, useful life, that when he was about to leave the region, an old pioneer, moved by powerful emotions of grief at parting from him, sought him out, and, throwing his brawny arms about the good man's neck, wept aloud. The ice of his reserve once broken, Mr. W. has since taken his place among Christian men at the East."

In the older settled portions of our country, the amenities of the heart, and the gentle fireside graces often bloom in beauty. But on the frontier, the stronger, more valiant traits are developed. Indeed, if it were not for woman, no new country could be civilized. It would be the old story of Adam and the beasts over again. Every thing would end in Crusoe experiments, in hunting and trapping, mining and fishing. Woman, however, has more than her share of work in reclaiming earth's wastes. I have visited many hundred cabin homes on the frontier, and my conclusion is, that to the wife and mother, more than to any other influence, belongs the credit of whatever of advancement is made socially. Encompassed with untold difficulties, she not only does her own work, but aids and encourages her husband in his. She helps build the cabin, "put up the fence," drive home the cows, take care of the crops, "fight the prairie fires," "tend" the store, keep the tavern, and take charge of the post-office.

There was Mrs. C., whom I first saw when going with a friend for family supplies. How I started back on entering "the store," supposing I had blundered into a private room. A bed, neatly covered, stood in a corner, a coffee-mill ready for use hung against the wall. These first met the eye. However, the sight of flour, and other articles of merchandise, reassured me. It was a two-roomed cabin, with a low sleeping apartment overhead. Yet in that little building a brisk trade was carried on, a number of boarders found accommodation, and the post-office was kept; and Mrs. C., to allow her husband leisure to put other "irons in the fire," superintended the whole, respected by all the settlers for her faultless judgment, and kind, dignified bearing.

So also woman's influence is felt in religious matters.

On account of the severity of the winter, our dwelling, being central, was for a time our sanctuary. One Sabbath morning, the mercury being thirty below zero, not a person came save two Christian ladies, who had walked nearly two miles to attend meeting! I had not felt inclined to chide our brethren for their absence, so fierce was the morning, and the courageous zeal of those devoted women filled me with admiration. The incident was characteristic.

And in the fearful national contest now raging, the women of our free frontier will not be found wanting. Their hearts took fire when Kansas was invaded by border ruffians. Not a few Southern ladies, brought up in luxury, have I met with in cabin homes, self-exiled from the places of their birth, by their abhorrence of American slavery. Prairie women, self-reliant, free in spirit as the air they breathe, have no affinity with tyrant traitors. And were it possible that through the sorcery of party politics, or some other fell influence, the fathers and brothers of the Northwest should falter in this struggle, the loyal mothers and sisters could not. Inspired by heroism, nursed by danger and deprivation, they would court any suffering or peril rather than see the fair structure of our civilization and freedom overthrown by the barbarized champions of human bondage.

THE MIDNIGHT CALL.

THE winter of 18— was marked with unusual severity. I remember it the more vividly because of the incident which follows.

One night I sat by the fire, absorbed in reading. It was just the evening to enjoy a good book and home comforts, for the storm, which had been raging through the day, and still whirling the snow against the windows, repressed all desire to go abroad, and shut out intruders. I read on, till, through the roar of the tempest, I heard the muffled tones of a neighboring church clock strike eleven. Another hour had nearly passed when I was aroused by a knock at the door, and, opening it, a woman, clad in a thin shawl covered with snow, came timidly in. Her eyes were swollen with weeping, and her whole appearance expressed deep sorrow.

Standing, and wringing her hands in her anguish, she said, —

"My father is dying! He is in great distress of body and mind. I've called to ask if you won't please come and see him, for there's no one to speak a word to him about his soul, and I fear he can't live till morning."

"But," said I, "I am not a minister, and am afraid I could be of little service. Has your father no experienced Christian friend who would like to converse with him? What church does he attend?"

"We do not go any where to meeting," she replied, with an embarrassed air; "but father had been talking about it some time!"

"Hadn't you better go for a clergyman, then? There's Rev. Mr. E."

"I've been for him," she quickly returned, "but he was not at home, and then I inquired for some one who could pray, and a man sent me to you. *Do* please go, sir, for father is very anxious that I get some one, and I can't leave him long, he suffers so, and he'll feel dreadfully if nobody comes to see him."

There was a coincidence in this unexpected call that impressed me. I had been much exercised with the desire to be more actively useful as a Christian, and had felt moved to pray that larger opportunities for doing good might be given. Was this an answer to that prayer? But it did not come in the way I had anticipated, and numberless excuses were ready to present themselves, the most weighty of which was my extreme youth, and consequent inexperience; and (shall I confess it?) I even glanced, with selfish shrinking, out at the driving blast. But the case would admit of no parleying. With pale, imploring face, my caller stood waiting my decision. Strength came, and I said, —

"I will go, and do the best I can for your father;" and, thanking me, she hurried away.

In a distant and disreputable part of the city, alone, on a dreary declivity overlooking the sea, stood the dwelling of the sick man. Entering, I had stepped to the feeble fire that flickered in the grate, to warm me ere speaking to him, when, casting my eyes toward the bed, they met his. Such an expression of wild despair I had never before seen. In the thrilling tones of one consciously approaching eternity unprepared, he exclaimed, stretching out his hand, —

"*I want some one to point me the way!*"

Instantly all diffidence fled; and, grasping his hand, I began to question him about his past life and present feelings. Suspicious of "death-bed repentance," I dealt plainly with him, which was well received. The result was a conviction that his was a case of genuine sorrow for sin. He had been a man of great physical strength and endurance. His business had called him to stand much in the water, as he worked about the vessels in the harbor, experiencing no ill effects from his exposed life till within a short time, when his lower limbs commenced swelling, accompanied by excruciating pain, the torture increasing as the disease crept up toward the vitals. Now his sufferings were well nigh intolerable, and his swollen appearance made him a truly frightful object. His naturally fine mind remained unclouded, however, and its whole vigor was exercised in self-accusing reviews of the past, and hopeless anticipations of the future.

"Oh," said he, "it's not the fear of death that troubles me so much as thoughts of my wasted, godless life. I have lived as if there was no God. What a stupid, ungrateful wretch I have been! And he has been so good, so forbearing, so patient. For fifty years and more I never saw a sick day, and yet no love toward him who made and preserved me! Oh, how can I think of it!"—and he covered his face as if to hide some hideous vision.

"But," I asked, "did you have no concern about these things till you were taken sick?"

"Yes; one day, a few weeks before, I fell to thinking over my past life, — I know not what made me, — and I saw it to be all wrong. Then I resolved to do better. But what a task I found it to overcome evil habits formed through so many years; and then my sins, my sins, they were a load crushing me to despair. One thing, however, I determined on, and that was to attend preaching somewhere. But, delaying to get suitable clothing, I was meanwhile laid up with this sickness. And now," he continued, "what I wish more than any thing else is to be rid of sin and serve God. But how can this be? How can I hope he will have mercy on me, when all the strength of my days has been given to self and sin? What shall I do? what shall I do? It's all dark to me."

Assuring him that salvation was free and ample, that the blessed Saviour invited all who felt their need of it to partake without money and without price, he could not credit the good news, and exclaimed, with moving earnestness, —

"Read it to me from *the Book*. I want to hear it for myself, that I may know there is no mistake about it!"

Drawing a Bible from my pocket, and lifting up a prayer for guidance, for I knew not where to turn, I opened at this passage: "Jesus stood and cried, saying, If any man thirst, let him come unto me and drink." A divine radiance seemed to rest on the Lord's invitation, and as I was explaining it, he suddenly exclaimed, —

"*I see it!*" He had fallen back on the pillow, a smile surpassingly beautiful irradiating his before distorted features. Those wondrous words of Christ, in which divine majesty blends with perfect human sympathy, through the Spirit's power, had inspired trust. The cloud, the darkness, the storm passed from his soul, and, like a tired infant nestling in his mother's arms, so he found rest in the love of his Saviour.

How blessed to kneel in prayer after such a change! Prayer was turned to praise, and that lowly cot became as the gate of heaven. Nor did his peace abate, for when I called again, three days afterwards, and inquired how he felt, —

"Oh!" said he, with beaming face, "it's so delightful; *it is peace in the morning, and peace at night.* My mind is so at rest," he continued, "that even my bodily pains, at times, seem all to have left me." But how can I express the gladness that filled my heart that night, as I left the aged convert to return home! The howling tempest could not drown the melody that came down from angel-harps, to the ear of faith, as in the presence of God there was joy over another repentant sinner. Christian disciple, pray to be a true laborer for Christ. Watch to improve each opportunity the Lord shall give for activity in his vineyard. Charlotte Elizabeth writes, "I asked work of my heavenly Master, and he gave it." None shall ask it of him in vain. Fear not to follow his leadings. The impenitent are more ready to hear on the subject of their eternal interests than is generally supposed. "I have," says Newcomb, "conversed with many hundreds, in almost every variety of states of mind, not excepting avowed infidels, but have rarely met with one who did not receive it kindly, and treat me with courtesy." Since the incident related above, which occurred in my eighteenth year, personal religious conversation with some *thousands* enables me to bear a similar testimony.

THE WORLD-WANDERER.

I WAS visiting in the quiet city of N——. On the street a clerical friend met me, and said,—

"I want you to come to our conference meeting this evening, and hear one of my members talk. It will do you good."

Now I confess to a partiality for those social services, in which young and old, the lettered and unlettered, all turn preachers, and in the freedom of God's family circle make heart-offerings of prayer, and praise, and exhortation. Would that we had less *pulpit* and more *church* in our sanctuaries; at least, I should prefer it.

The good pastor's flock were accustomed to prayer-meeting privileges, and no time was lost.

"That's the man," whispered my friend; "listen."

At that instant a man arose in a side pew, and commenced speaking. Partly bald, his thin, light hair fell from a high forehead, while his sharply cut features, bronzed by exposure to sun and storm, wore a bold, stern look, as of one accustomed to face danger without shrinking. His voice was resonant and full, his manner assured and forcible. A tender smile, like sunlight resting on the jagged rock, played over his face, — a face accustomed more to harsher moods, one would think.

His words — I will not attempt to rehearse them — were wondrously weighty and convincing, as, with a confidence such as the Apostles had after the baptism of Pentecost, he reasoned out of the Scriptures of "righteousness, temperance, and judgment to come." He spoke like one who had consciously emerged from darkness to light; who had been soundly converted from the extremity of ungodliness to a living discipleship. And when he alluded to his own experience, how touching and persuasive!

"Sinner!" he exclaimed; "you who make light of these things, pleased with the trifles of earth, hugging sin, your deadliest foe, to your hearts, rejecting the only good, eagerly pressing on the broad road to destruction, look at me, a monument of God's sparing mercy, a trophy of his grace! Some of you have known me from my childhood. You can remember what a vile, God-defying, blasphemous wretch I was. You have heard me insult the Majesty of heaven and earth; yes, pour out my swearing wrath on Him who died for me. It is but a year since he spoke to me as to Saul of Tarsus, and brought me to his feet. Since then my testimony has been one and the same. I am a new creature; old things have passed away. I have found him of whom Moses and the prophets did write; and in finding him I have found every thing. Sin's strong fetters have been broken; pardon, peace, joy, love, the fellowship of the saints, the communion of the Holy Ghost, heaven, all are mine, and can *you* stay away?" Then, plaintively, almost soliloquizing, "Fifty years of my life were wasted in sin, before I saw the great light. I have been all over the world, seen hardships and danger in many a clime, all the while defy ing the God who made and preserved me. Yes, I have been to Palestine, trodden that sacred soil with a heart harder than adamant, gone over those places hallowed by the weary feet, watered by the tears and blood of Immanuel,— but what was it all to me? Oh, that I could once more see that land, all-glorious! Oh, that I might again look on Jordan and Tiberias, Gethsemane and Calvary, now that he has had pity on a wretch like me, and revealed himself to my soul. How dear, how holy, would be those scenes!— what joy, what rapture would thrill my heart! But this can not be. But, blessed be God, the heavenly Canaan

'Stands dressed in living green.'

I shall see *that*. I shall behold Him whom I once reviled, but who is now to my soul the chiefest among ten thousand, and the One altogether lovely. Sinner, will you go with me? Come, for there is room for all!"

"What," said the preacher, as we walked home together, "did you think of that?" referring to the exhortation I have meagerly sketched.

"Ah!" I replied, with a sigh, "if we all could speak with that assurance of faith and depth of conviction."

"And yet," he continued, "that man was one of the worst, most hopeless scoffers I ever heard of. The language he would use in expressing his scorn and hatred of the Saviour is too horrible to repeat. But since his conversion not an opposer dares breathe an accusation against his demeanor. Having been forgiven much, he loves much."

"What were the circumstances connected with his conversion?"

"A member of my church and Sabbath school," said he, "was in search of scholars. She was looking for them among the poor and neglected. She had heard of this man — was aware that he was a skeptic of the blackest hue; but knowing that he had children growing up untaught in divine things, her heart was moved with pity; and, repressing her timidity, she begged leave for them to attend Sunday school. Her conciliatory, persevering efforts, were rewarded by her request being granted. The youngest of them, a little girl of five, became religiously impressed, and began the habit of secret prayer. One evening, just at dark, her father chancing to pass the door of her room, thought he heard a voice. It was little Mary offering her childish petitions. Just then she was asking God to bless and save her dear father. The listening parent heard his name thus laid before the mercy-seat. Conviction followed. 'What does this mean?' he ejaculated. 'My little girl praying for me! Am I, then, such a sinner?' His life came up for review; he was plunged in wretchedness, could not sleep, and next morning sent for me. He was walking the room, gloomy and agitated, as I entered.

"'Sir,' said he, 'can you prove that the Bible is true?'

"'Yes, to one who is candid,' I answered.

"'Then let me hear your arguments,' he rejoined.

"I spent the day with him. Ere I left, at his request I prayed for him, and he broke out in earnest supplication for himself. When light dawned, his mind was flooded. No doubts have distressed him since. His testimonies always have power with unbelievers; they don't question the change. But did you observe," he added, "how he yearned to see the Holy Land once more? He often reverts to that, reproaching himself for his indifference and unbelief when there."

The converted infidel died about a year after. His last moments were glorious. Denied another sight of the earthly Canaan, the heavenly soon burst upon his enraptured vision.

Oh, ye laborers in the Sabbath schools of our land, go forth! Go forth into the highways and hedges, into the homes of error, the dens of corruption, and bear thence the tender child where hallowed influences descend, and the knowledge that maketh wise unto salvation is imparted. Save the children, and it may be you will save the fathers and the mothers, who, transformed, shall become champions of the cross.

16

THE PASTOR'S DREAM.

Deacon G. was a pillar in the —— church some years since. He was the very embodiment of good deaconly qualities; — bland, zealous, prayerful, efficient. His hospitable doors were ever open to the "pilgrim and stranger," and many a weary man of God, and many a hungry wanderer, was sheltered and fed beneath his roof. And not seldom did some struggling theological student, visiting him of a vacation, have his fundless wallet replenished, and his outer man improved by the exchange of his worn boots and threadbare coat for a more comely and comfortable garb. It was whispered around, however, that with all his virtues, he had one weakness. He was pronounced prodigal in his alms-deeds, by some of the more "prudent," and the pastor inclined to the opinion. He admired the whole-hearted benevolence of the deacon, but being himself more wary, and having his friend's interests really at heart, he became much troubled about the matter. For some time he revolved the subject in silence, until compelled, as he thought, by a sense of duty, he waited on his official helper to express his concern. He laid before him all his fears, endeavoring, with a discriminating hand, to draw the line between a safe and an imprudent generosity.

"Have I not enough for the support of my family? Do I at all distress them by giving away?" asked the deacon. "This may be true," said the minister, "but many of your brethren fear for the future for you. You know not what reverses may await you. Is it not wise; do you not owe it to your family so to husband your resources as to be prepared for emergencies that may arise?"

His listener duly weighed each word, but was scarcely convinced of the necessity of the caution. It seemed to him that he had only given of his abundance, and that a watchful Providence had granted him to reap liberally as he sowed liberally.

The pastor left; his solicitude somewhat softened, perhaps, by the interview; yet with the consciousness that he had relieved himself of any responsibility in whatever might befall the deacon's worldly affairs, while the latter remained with his large heart uncontracted.

That night the pastor dreamed that, taking his daily walk, he bent his steps to the sea-side. It was a bright day in summer, and he paused to look on the broad expanse. Soft clouds lay dreamily against the horizon. Sea-birds sailed slowly through the air, or darted down upon their finny prey. The white-crested waves flashed back golden rays. While absorbed in the glorious scene, a step behind caused him to turn his head, and he saw Deacon G. approaching. The latter appeared not to notice him, but stepping to the verge of the shore, took from a basket on his arm loaf after loaf of wholesome looking bread, and tossed them into the water.

"Stop! stop!" exclaimed the pastor, in surprise, "why this waste?"

The deacon pointed solemnly into the sea, and said, "Look! observe!"

The former looked, and, to his astonishment, saw that for each loaf thrown in, the returning wave brought back a basketful, and cast them at the donor's feet!

In great wonder he awoke, and the next day calling on the deacon, related his dream, and added, tearfully,—

"Go on, brother! go on! Cast your bread upon the waters — doubtless, after many days, it will be returned to you!"

A SMILE, A GLANCE, A HYMN.

A THOUGHTLESS boy of fifteen, who had heard the Bible and the Christian profession treated lightly, imbibed the poison of skepticism. He had come to think that religion was only a name, and that the followers of Christ were a gloomy people, denying themselves this world's enjoyments and receiving no equivalent. It chanced one day that he was sent on an errand to a lady, of whom his parents would often speak compassionately, as one who had but a little while to live.

"Poor Mrs. S.," they were wont to exclaim, "how dreadful must it be to her to know that she must leave her beautiful home, her babe and husband. But," they would add, "she is a church-member,— wonder of she is sustained in her great trouble."

The son called on Mrs. S. With pleased emotions, for he was a lad of fine taste, he looked at the dwelling and out-grounds. Wealth had here lavished its stores in adorning and furnishing a home where, it would seem, scarcely a wish was ungratified. The garden was a paradise of rare plants and flowers. Within, the foot pressed the richest carpets, luxurious chairs and lounges invited repose, while the elegant library contained the choicest productions in literature. A fair babe, the picture of health, lay sleeping in its pretty cot. He glanced at the costly house and dimpled child, and then at the sick woman, and thought how terrible a thing it is to die amid such scenes. He expected that the countenance of the death-doomed wife and mother would reflect his feelings. But no. That saintly expression, such as beautifies those only who have been purified by suffering, and "look not at the things that are seen and temporal, but at the things that are unseen and eternal," lighted up her face. An ever-present smile, sweet and heavenly beyond any thing he had ever seen, spoke of her deep, spiritual joy. It overwhelmed him with surprise. "This, this," said an inward voice, "is what Christianity does for Death's victims!" There is, there must be, he felt, reality in that which can give happiness under circum stances so forbidding. That smile followed him, an unanswerable witness for Jesus, till he was led to seek the dying Christian's Saviour. "A smile — a simple smile convinced me," he would afterwards say.

In a rural town in Maine lived a Mr. B., an openly irreligious man. His custom was, when his neighbors were at public worship on the Lord's day, to take his fishing-rod or gun, and stroll about the fields and woods in search of amusement. One hot summer day, starting on his accustomed ramble, his course led him by the village church. The pastor, a devoted, godly minister, now in glory, had just risen to name his text. The Sabbath-breaker passed on ere it was announced. But the door of the sanctuary being open on account of the heat, his glance within met that of the man of God. Those calm, unworldly eyes, with their "holy expression," as the transgressor subsequently stated, shot conviction to his heart, and he found no peace till he found it beneath the sin-atoning cross.

A faithful pastor,* who made much of
"the lambs," was in the habit of taking
a little girl, the daughter of a parishioner,
on his knee when he called, and teaching
her a hymn to sing. He taught her those
lines from Watts, commencing,

"Earth has engrossed my love too long."

She had a clear, rich voice, and when
the family would sing those words her bird-
like notes might be heard above all the
rest. One day she came in from play, hot
and fevered — scarlet fever had seized her,
and she soon faded from earth, to be folded
in the arms of the "chief Shepherd."
Many years passed. With her death the
stanzas ceased to be sung and were seldom thought of. An older brother, who
had grown to manhood, read infidel books,

---

* Rev. J. Newton Brown.

forsook the house of God, and became a caviller at religion. His business called him to a distant town, and having a taste for music, he became a member of a choir, still unchanged in his feelings towards Christianity. One Sabbath the officiating clergyman gave out the hymn already referred to. While engaged in singing it, suddenly he seemed to hear that child-voice ringing out, in cadences of angelic sweetness, her favorite lines, —

> "Earth has engrossed my love too long;
> 'Tis time I lift mine eyes
> Upward, dear Father, to thy throne,
> And to my native skies."

Each word uttered with thrilling distinctness to his ear, he was lifted above his skepticism, heaven became a reality, the gospel a divine power. Overcome by emotion, he sat down before the song had

ended, — melted, subdued, humbled, tearful.
After his conversion he would often allude
to that hour as one of deep and vivid impression. Little did that loving pastor
think what he was doing for that brother
when the fair-haired girl sat in his lap committing those verses.

A LOST OPPORTUNITY.

I HAD been invited to preach for a few Sabbaths in a pleasant village on the seaboard. During services, on my first Sunday's labors, my attention was attracted to a tall, rough-looking man, of pale countenance, on my right. Each time I glanced in his direction I saw that his eyes were fixed upon me, as if he were intent to hear, and yet with an expression that betokened any thing but sympathy with the truths of the gospel. There was nothing in his personal appearance that would lead one to single him from the throng of strangers in the sanctuary, yet anxiety for his spiritual good arose in my heart, and during the succeeding week I experienced a solicitude in his behalf that could only express itself in prayer. Next Sabbath, on my return, the stranger occupied the same seat, and while preaching I often felt for him an interest so peculiar that I resolved to seek an interview for religious conversation. Lingering to speak with Christian friends, he had retired from the congregation before I had put my resolution in practice.

"Who is the tall man that sat in the third slip on my right?" I asked of a lady resident of the place.

"Oh," she replied, "that's Mr. L., a poor, wretched infidel, who don't believe in the Bible, nor even that there is a God. A fearfully violent and blasphemous opposer of religion, I can't imagine how he happened to come to church to-day; he has not been within a Christian sanctuary for years."

"It is singular, but without any knowledge of his condition, I have felt an earnest desire to speak to him on the subject of his soul's salvation. How do you think he would receive it?"

"He would swear at you terribly, I fear. Why, that man will stand up, and dare God to strike him dead!"

"Is it possible?"

"Yes, and what makes his case worse is, he has a bad cough that may end in consumption. When a coughing-fit comes on it puts him in a rage, that vents itself in the most shocking oaths."

What I heard respecting the man of itself would not have disheartened me. But there was such a thing, I remembered, as casting "pearls before swine," and impressions were so trustless. Therefore, I deferred calling upon him, as I had designed, that week; however, I was unhappy from a conviction of neglected duty that no reasoning could remove. Wherever I went, however occupied, his pale face would haunt me, and mentioning the case to a Christian acquaintance, united prayer was frequently offered for his conversion. I had determined to speak with him the next Sabbath without fail. But he was not in his place. My engagements were such that I could not conveniently visit him at his home. Another week rolled by, and he was still missing.

"Where is Mr. L.?" I inquired, of the friend before alluded to; "I *must* see him. I believe the Holy Spirit is impressing his case upon my soul, and I shall not find peace till I have one faithful talk with him, whether he repulses me or not."

"Ah, sir," was the reply, "you are too late!"

"Too late! What do you mean?" I asked, tremblingly.

"He is dead!"

"Dead?"

"Yes, his end was dreadful. A week ago last Thursday night he was sitting, conversing with his wife, when, she says, something internal seemed to break, sounding like the running down of a clock. Instantly he sprang to his feet, exclaiming, '*My time has come!*' then sinking on his knees, he cried to God for mercy. His shrieks were heard by neighbors living far away. In a few moments all was over,— he had breathed his last!"

The intelligence smote heavily on my heart, filling me with an agony almost too keen to be borne.

"Oh," I cried, "would that I had yielded to the Spirit, and not lingered to question and doubt. Oh, that I had spoken one word to him concerning his need of Christ!" I then related, with shame and confusion of face, all my exercises in relation to the deceased.

"Strange," said my friend; "but that man talked much about you the last week or two, and always in your favor. He uttered not a word against your preaching. I know not but he would have welcomed any thing you might have said to him."

He had heard something of the gospel those two Sabbaths; he had not scorned what he heard; united intercession had been made for him; he had cried for mercy at last; there was a gleam of comfort in these reflections, but oh, what would I not have given to have had some testimony from his own lips that he had renounced atheism, and cast himself on the grace of the compassionate Saviour!

Christian reader, our fathers and mothers in Israel believed in the office-work of the Holy Spirit; believed that he moved on the hearts in which he dwelt to special labor for perishing souls. Have we not wandered away from their simple, scriptural faith, and thus grieved the Holy Comforter, and become unfruitful in the work of the Lord, till it is to be feared that the blood of souls may be found on our garments? Oh, if you would never know the bitter sorrow that to this day overwhelms me, as Memory recalls that poor skeptic, yield to the heavenly guidance, and fear not to speak when the Spirit prompts.

"NOT IN VAIN."

"My first sermon," said a pastor, "what a vivid recollection I have of it!" A ministerial acquaintance who was to spend the Sabbath from home, on exchange, had invited me to ride with him to his appointment. On arriving, he said,—

"I shall depend on you to preach half the day."

The afternoon was left for me to improve. There was a heavy rain, and few ventured out, for which I felt more and more thankful as the services advanced. My discourse, partly written and partly extempore, sounded to my own ears like the "foolishness of preaching" indeed; and with an inward resolution never again to commit the folly of speaking from the sacred desk, I went home mortified, humbled, and desponding.

Some years afterwards, while settled over a church in Connecticut, an acute bilious attack laid me by for a few weeks from the labors of the pastorate. One day, while lying dejected on the sick-bed, a stranger visited me. He was also a pastor, residing some twelve miles away. After some pleasant, preliminary words, he said, —

"I have come on an errand to you. It is a message intrusted to me by a dying woman. Do you remember spending a Sabbath in H—— some years ago, in company with Rev. Mr. F.?"

"I do," said I, while a quick flush passed over my face.

"Do you recollect what a great rain

there was, and how thin the attendance?"

"I could not forget it if I would."

"Well," said he, "I was pastor of that church then; we did not meet, however. Two years after you were there, I was sent for to converse with a lady about to die. She was ready for the messenger. 'But,' said she, 'I have a special request to make of you;' then, referring to your sermon, at that time, as being wonderfully blest to her, she added, 'I fear he went away discouraged, supposing he had done no good; and I want you to tell him how God sent home that discourse to my soul, that he may know that his labor was not in vain in the Lord.' And," continued my thoughtful caller, "hearing you were sick, and fearing you might feel low-spirited in being unable to discharge your accustomed duties, I felt it my duty to ride over and deliver my message now, hoping it would cheer you in your afflictions."

"My word shall not return unto me void," says Jehovah. Toil on with courage, all you who cultivate the harvest-field of the gospel here. In a world of clearer light you shall reap in joy!

THE PRAYING BANKRUPT.

SOME twenty-five years since, in a seaport town in New England, there resided a deacon, who was engaged in lucrative business. Although of prudent habits, his benevolence led him to indorse largely for one who had won his confidence as a Christian brother, but afterwards proved to be a designing knave. This issued in the good deacon's failure, when, with scrupulous integrity, every thing that could be claimed by his creditors was given up. A winter of great severity and of general business depression followed. His wife and young children looked to him for a subsistence which he knew not how to furnish, as his most diligent efforts for employment were unsuccessful.

A debt incurred, with no prospect of payment, was, in his estimation, sin; and he sadly saw their little stock of provisions rapidly diminishing, with no way to obtain more. He was a man of prayer as well as action, and carried the case to Him who feedeth the ravens. Yet long, weary weeks passed and no succor came. At length the morning dawned when the last stick of wood was on the fire, and little Hatty told her father that the candles were all gone; "and how," asked she, "shall we take care of dear mamma to-night?"

The question went to the father's heart with dagger-like poignancy. The vision of his suffering wife, gasping her life away in the last fearful stages of consumption, her comfortless sick-room unwarmed, unlighted, and the thick darkness which he knew would enshroud her mind, when made aware of the extent of their destitution, would have driven him to distraction, were it not that he yet had hope in One mighty to save. He fled to his closet, and there, in an agony of prayer, besought the Lord for help; and, forgetting all other wants, plead and plead again for the two articles now specially needed, specifying them with reiterated earnestness. He arose from his knees in full assurance of faith and with heavenly tranquillity, and went forth, expecting deliverance, looking for it, however, in but one way, — through his own earnings. But after a fruitless day of seeking employment, gloomily he returned home.

He entered his gate, and was startled to see before him a generous pile of wood.

Little Johnny opened the door, clapping his hands, exclaiming, —

"Oh, pa! we've got some wood and some candles!"

"But where did you get them? Are you sure they were not left here by mistake?"

"Oh, no, pa!" interrupted Hatty, "they were not left by mistake. A man knocked at the door with his whip, and when I opened it, he asked if you lived here. I told him you did. Then he said, 'Here are some candles and a load of wood for him.'"

"I asked him if you sent them, and he said, 'I rather guess your pa don't know any thing about it.'"

"Who did send them, then?" said I.

"'Oh,' said he, 'I musn't tell, but you may say to your father that they are a present.'"

But to what instrumentality they were indebted for the relief was a mystery. And what particularly interested Deacon P. was, the character of the anonymous presents; that the very things so much needed, and no others, should be sent, and he was sure he had mentioned his want of them to no human ear.

He questioned the children anew. They described the man who knocked at the door, the horse and truck he drove. A new thought struck him. "Why," said he, "that team belongs to my old enemy, Graff. Can it be possible he is the donor? If so, surely the finger of God has touched his heart." Deacon P. was, however, so convinced that he was their benefactor, that he resolved on an immediate call on that gentleman.

But who was Mr. Graff?

Some years before, the sacredness of the Sabbath was openly violated by a brisk trade in fish. The hundreds of boatmen, sailors, and their friends, engaged in this desecration, were so potent in influence, that nobody thought of risking interference. Deacon P., though a man of peace, was also a man of moral courage. He determined to put a stop to the iniquity. His friends warned him that his life would be endangered; but, at first alone, and afterward with a brother deacon, he would take a walk along the wharves of a Sunday morning to ascertain who broke the laws by traffic on that day. Men swore at him like fiends, fired his dwelling at several different times, and at last "bound themselves with an oath" to kill him. Yet they feared his presence, and at his approach stores would be deserted of customers, and closed with great celerity. This species of Sabbath-breaking was at length broken up, after various hairbreadth escapes on the part of Deacon P. and his compatriot, the authorities being shamed into action by their fearless zeal.

The brutal drunkenness of the sailors, and the degradation and suffering of their families, with which Deacon P. was in this enterprise brought into contact, opened his eyes to the evils of the liquor traffic; and turning over his Sabbath reform to the legal authorities, he became known as a temperance advocate. This also brought him enemies, sometimes changing even friends into foes. Distiller Graff was among the latter, from a warm friend becoming bitterly alienated. In vain did the grieved deacon strive to conciliate by explanation and personal kindness. Even the trifling civility of a bow was rudely unnoticed by Mr. Graff.

Deacon P. entered the distillery of his old friend. For the first time for years its proprietor looked up with a nod and smile of recognition. It was evident something unusual had softened his heart.

"I have called," said the deacon, "to ask if you can tell me who sent some wood and candles to my house to-day?"

"Yes, sir, I sent them."

"You are very kind; but pray tell me how you came to do so?"

"But first, let me inquire if you really needed them?"

"Oh, I can not express to you how much!"

"Well, then, I suppose I must explain," said Mr. Graff. "It's all very singular, and sometimes seems very foolish. This morning, about ten o'clock, as I was busy at my work, suddenly a voice seemed to say to me, '*Send some wood to Deacon P., he is in want!*' I was astonished. I could not believe you needed it. And I could not send it to *you* of all others. I tried to banish the thought, and went to work again more earnestly. But the voice — it seemed within me — said again, with painful distinctness, '*Send some wood to Deacon P., he is in want!*' I scouted the idea as weak and silly; a mere phantasy of the brain; but it was of no use; I had to succumb. The more I ridiculed and fought it, the more vivid and irresistible was the impression, until, to purchase peace, and in some awe, I confess, I bade John load his team with wood and leave it at your door.

"For a moment I was at rest; but only

for a moment. The imperative whisper came, '*Send some candles!*' Said I to myself, this is too absurd; I will not gratify this whim; but again I was so beset with the mandate, and so distressed and baffled in repelling it, that, as a cheap way to get out of torment, I handed John a package of candles also.

"This matter has been in my mind ever since. Sometimes I have thought it almost a freak of insanity, and then again, such was the strange character of the impression, so unexpected, so solemn and powerful, and such the singular peace following compliance with its dictates, that I almost believe it to be supernatural."

"It is, indeed, the doings of Him who is wonderful in working," replied Deacon P. "It was about ten o'clock, I well remember, that I plead with God for the very articles you sent me, in an agony of wrestling I never knew before. It was then too that my soul was filled with the conviction that my prayer was heard and relief would come."

Since hearing a venerated relative relate this incident in his own life, we have often wondered how the skeptic can dispose of such occurrences. While it would be presumption for the believer to expect to live by prayer alone, to be fed without his own coöperation, as was Elijah, yet are there not events happening all along the history of the church, in the experiences of individual members, to be accounted for only on the ground of a special Providence, regardful of the emergencies of the believing, suffering people of God? Surely, "light is sown for the righteous," and to them,

"The deepest dark reveals the starriest hope."

"A SOFT ANSWER."

It was in the town of ——, Connecticut, in which I began my never-to-be-forgotten labors, distributing religious reading, and urging the messages of salvation on all I met, as I visited from house to house.

"If you wish to see the most discouraging features of your mission at the outset, visit the Northeast District," a clergyman had said to me; "every thing that is bad you will find there. I hope it will not discourage you."

"I had made out, by the aid of Christian friends, a moral and religious chart of the place, by sketching on paper the streets and roads, with the names of the families living on them, together with such information about the spiritual condition of the inhabitants as I needed to guide conversation.

Among the residents was a Mr. D., who was represented to be a bold, swearing man, high-tempered, and abusive to those of evangelical faith. He had once belonged to a Christian church, but getting into difficulty with some of the members, he became imbittered, and ceased to attend the meetings, even on the Sabbath. Ere long he took to drinking, became profane, would work at his trade on the Lord's day, himself and his numerous household becoming openly hostile to the interests of religion, and advocates of the doctrine of Universalism.

Such was the account of him as given me by his grieved pastor, and others of his former friends, who had long since given up all hope of his restoration.

Mr. D. I found at his blacksmith's shop, a brawny, dark-browed man. He was blowing at the bellows. Approaching him with my basket on my arm, I said,—

"I have called, sir, with some choice books and tracts; would you like one?"

The old man turned upon me in a tempest of passion.

"What did you bring your miserable fire-and-brimstone trash here for?" pouring forth a torrent of coarse and insulting appellatives.

Waiting till the ebullition subsided, I gently said,— for a rising pity overpowered all natural resentments,—

"I ask your pardon, sir; I did not design to intrude on you, but knowing that the works I have are the productions of

A Soft Answer. Frontier. p. 278.

some of the best minds, and that they are intended to benefit those who read them, I ventured to offer them to you."

He stood silent a moment. Then, softened, said,—

"I will buy one of them;" and taking up the first volume that came to hand,— a work on the Sabbath,— left a piece of silver in its place, and returned to his task.

"I heard that you called on Mr. D. at his shop," said the good minister to me, next day; "how did he receive you?"

I described the interview. By way of comment, he said,—

"Well, the book he purchased was just what he needed. I hope he will read it, but I fear he will not."

Three months after, as I was passing through the place, I called again on the clergyman.

"I have a desire to know," said I, "if you have seen any fruits of my labor in your parish?"

"Yes," he replied, with a pleased smile, "I have. My congregation has been larger since, than for years. And," he added, "do you remember Mr. D., the blacksmith, who treated you so outrageously, but relented, and bought a little treatise on the Sabbath? What was my astonishment, a few Sundays after, to see that man and all his family come into church! They have been regular attendants ever since."

Not long after I was permitted to hear that the blacksmith, reclaimed from his backslidings, had been restored to membership, and that a number of his children had professed Christ before the world.

THAT PROMISE.

At a recent Sabbath school concert the superintendent said, "We have no speakers from abroad to announce this evening, and therefore we shall have to rely for remarks on our *home* gifts. I see that brother S. is present. We would like to hear from him."

The person named, a young man, came immediately forward, and said, in substance, —

"Some years ago I made a promise. It was, that whenever I should be invited to speak a word for Christ, in public, I would make no excuses, but do the best I could. That promise I have ever regarded as sacred, because it is a promise, and because it was made to my nearest and best Friend. Once I was in fearful danger. He rescued me from that danger. Once I was wretched, without peace of mind, unhappy, degraded. He raised me up from my low estate, comforted and cheered me. Many times since then I have been in trouble and he has helped me. I have sometimes forgotten that Friend, often grieved him, said and done things that were displeasing to him, slighted and insulted him in ways that no other friend could overlook, and yet he has been constantly kind, forbearing, and generous. All I have that is worth any thing I owe to his love, and all I expect that is desirable and glorious he only can give me. Can you tell me, children, who that Friend is?"

"Jesus! Jesus!" responded a score of voices.

"Yes, dear scholars," he replied, "it was Jesus; and I can not break my promise to such a Friend. Therefore it is that, though called upon unexpectedly, I will try to interest you for a few moments." And as he proceeded with his remarks— apt, sprightly, impressive, it was plain that that Friend was true to his promise, and was furnishing him richly for that time of need.

And in thus redeeming our Christian pledge are we not always blest?

A Christian gentleman, whose "praise is in all the churches," not only for his large-hearted benevolence, but for his excellent gifts in prayer and exhortation, when a young convert, would be so embarrassed, when attempting to speak in conference meeting, as to be obliged to resume his seat almost without uttering a word. But he had resolved to persevere; he kept his resolution and excelled in these services.

A godly deacon, now seventy-five years of age, leads the devotions of the largest assemblies in and out of the denomination, and expounds Scripture with remarkable acceptance. Yet when a young man his speech was awkward and blundering, and his diffidence extreme. He was so illiterate also, that before reading a chapter in the Bible, in the presence of others, his wife had first to read it to him.

"I made a promise," said he, "when the Lord forgave my sins, that I would never refuse to speak for him, or to pray in public, when properly requested to do so, and I have kept my word."

Christian reader, have you made a similar promise? Have you kept it?

AFTER MANY DAYS.

Deacon N. held to both tables of the law, and when an object of charity presented itself, he was quite sure to "lend something" to the Lord. One evening a poorly-dressed sailor called at his door with a story of sorrow. He said he had been shipwrecked, and lost every thing but the scanty clothing he wore; was without money, food, or shelter. He was an entire stranger, and presented an appearance of extreme wretchedness; but the worthy deacon took him in, gave him a comfortable supper and bed, fitted him out with coat, pants, and vest, put some of the needful in his empty wallet, and then setting out with him in search of employment, secured a place for him on board a merchant-ship, and bade him good-by, amid a profusion of blessings and praises. It was a benevolent experiment, and many were the evil prophesyings of neighbors and friends concerning the issue of the case.

"I shall never forget your kindness," said the sailor, "and some day you shall hear from me again, and know that it has not been thrown away."

Years passed. The kind-hearted deacon failed in business, and removed to a distant town. But if worldly reverses had come, the richer blessings of the gospel were lavished with divine generosity on his household. One after another of his children was made the subject of renewing grace, till all were found walking in the commandments and ordinances of the Lord.

"Two of his sons entered the ministry. In the providence of God one of them was called to spend a Sabbath in the city of B——. During the evening discourse his attention was attracted to a well-dressed, intelligent looking man, whose eyes were fixed on his with marked interest. After service the stranger said, "May I ask, sir, if your name is N.?"

On receiving an answer in the affirmative, he exclaimed, with deep emotion, "God bless you, sir! I knew you from your resemblance to your father. You do not remember me, for you were a little boy when I came to his house, a cast-away sailor, ragged and hungry, without a cent in my pocket. He helped me when others looked at me with suspicion and turned me away unfed. I have never forgotten him, and never shall. Tell him I think of him often, and pray for him, too."

And as the grateful seaman departed, the generous bank bill that remained in the preacher's hand attested the sincerity of his words.

MY COUSIN.

AMIABLE and engaging, she was the life of the circles in which she moved. In personal attractions few were her equals, and from her kind and genial presence depression and gloom fled like darkness before the footsteps of morning. Her opening years were full of gladness; who could foresee that her "days of darkness would be many?"

George Evans had won her affections, and well do I remember my desire, though then a mere lad, to know the successful competitor for her hand. I first saw him under circumstances which filled me with apprehension. It was the anniversary of our national independence. He was passing with a crowd when a companion pointed him out. I followed him in anxious curiosity; for it seemed to me that he who was to wed my cousin Carrie should be nearly perfect. Many times did I wish myself far away, as, fascinated by a horror-struck interest, I was jostled in that throng, to hear from his lips the language of profanity, and witness proofs of his intemperance. Was *she* to be the wife of such a man? Friends had warned him of his evil habits, but he was so manly in appearance, and in her presence so correct in language and deportment, her attendant at church, and manifesting there such a reverence for religion, that she entertained no misgivings.

They were married. A year elapsed, during which nothing served to mar the happiness of the young couple, and we had well nigh dismissed our fears, when, one autumn evening, in passing their residence I met them. They had just returned from a walk, and were parting at the door. . "You will not stay late, will you, George?" Carrie was saying. I saw that she was pale. The husband gave an evasive reply, and left her. My direction lay with his, and as I followed on, the sorrowful pallor of her face haunted me. Conspicuous on a public corner was one of those gilded hells, which allure to destruction. Evans lingered a moment at the door, then passed hastily down the steps into the "saloon." The power of that infernal magic by which a man of reason is moved to prefer the orgies of such a mystery of iniquity, and the pestilential companionship of bloated, blasphemous wretches, to the society of the fair and pure being to whom he is united in holiest bonds, thank God, I know not; but this I know, that the stricken wife kept vigils of agony through that long night, and when the faithless husband returned, it was with unsteady step and brutal oaths. This was "but the beginning of sorrows." A friend thus gives a glimpse of her eventful history.

"You ask after Carrie Carleton. Poor woman, hers has been a sad lot. Her husband has dragged her down the steeps of misfortune, until worn and weary, Consumption has smitten her, and she weeps on the verge of the grave. Weeps, did I say? Yes, for him, but as for herself, she trusts all in the hands of her Saviour. What a miracle is love when hallowed and refined by piety! Of high family, and nurtured tenderly, yet allied by marriage to a sot and a tyrant, it is impossible to paint what she has so uncomplainingly endured. Some three years since a hollow cough, and frequent bleeding from the lungs admonished that her trials would be short. Physicians gave her up. But see how, at the mercy of circumstances, we are in this world. Evans, under the labors of the Washingtonians, reformed. For a time he seemed a man again, was frugal, industrious, and kind. But, insidiously tempted, he tasted again the enchanted cup, and sank lower than before. During his reformation Carrie became like one raised from the dead; her step regained its elasticity, and her laugh its gladness. She attributed this to a change of medicine, but when George again fell, she declined rapidly. His course in the downward road was fearfully accelerated. His business neglected, his credit gone, his days spent in the tippling-shop, and his nights in haunts of iniquity, on her devolved the sustenance of the family. This she worked hard to provide by taking boarders. But who would long remain to witness her sorrows, and to share her ill-treatment at the hands of her ill-clad, profane, and fault-finding companion? So, in a miserable chamber, Carrie toiled with her needle, solicitous for her husband when away, lest in the helplessness of inebriety, or in some drunken brawl, injury would come to him, or he commit some horrid crime.

It was affecting, amid all these hardships, to see how uncomplaining was the wife. When others censured his conduct she would make excuses for him, striving to make it appear that he was not so bad as they thought, or that his evil deeds were attributable to the influence of others.

Once only did she speak at all freely of her sufferings. It was when visiting at good deacon J.'s. After the family had retired, overburdened with anguish, she poured into the ears of the deacon and his sympathizing wife such a tale of neglect, anxiety, deprivation, and abuse, as well nigh broke their hearts.

"And why don't you leave such a monster forever?" said Mrs. J., her eyes streaming with tears.

"Oh!" she mournfully returned, "you can not tell what you would do as a drunkard's wife." Then added, rising and wringing her hands, "I love George, with all his faults! There's no living with him, and there's no living without him!"

Some time after, when visiting in a seaboard city, incidentally I learned that Mrs. Evans resided there. I found her in an obscure tenement. She welcomed me with a placid smile, — but how changed! so thin and wasted, — while on her cheeks bloomed the fatal crimson. The bare floor and meager furniture bespoke her destitution. In full prospect of death she conversed calmly of her tribulations, anticipating with hope the coming of the last messenger. More than a year previous, her husband deserted her on the pretense of going South for business. No tidings had she heard of him, though she diligently searched the papers and inquired at the post-office; faithful to him, though worse than widowed.

"And how have your little family managed to get along during this hard winter?"

"I have endeavored not to afflict others with our troubles," she replied, "but God has raised us up benefactors. And in the way in which this has been done I have realized how he would learn us, to the last, lessons of charity toward all. I have long been prejudiced against the Friends; but one stormy day, when the streets were blocked with snow, and we were very destitute, one of their number called. I was a little startled when he entered, but beneath his broad-brimmed hat was a face so benign, that I quickly forgot he was a stranger, and before I was aware he knew something of our necessities. Why, he seemed like my buried father! 'Thee mustn't suffer,' said he; and since, in our moments of extremity, when others would not venture to come, through the fiercest storms and the bitterest cold, and just when I had been praying with the most urgent sense of need, he, or his lovely wife, would be sure to happen in with a load of blessings. Now they are to me as angels of mercy, and even their peculiar garb seems beautiful, and their thee and thou are like music to my heart. Thus does our Father teach us to love all his children ere we meet them in his house above. And thus does he cause strangers to be as parents, when the nearest and dearest forsake us."

When the balmy south wind unlocked the frozen earth, and hailed by blithe songsters, the dead plant awoke to beauty and fragrance, Carrie Carleton found the repose of the grave.

> "Asleep in Jesus! blessed sleep!
> From which none ever wake to weep."

Though slain by the treachery of man, through the " Faithful and True," she conquered death, and welcomed the tomb with a smile of joy.

My murdered cousin! I think of thee in the night watches, and weep at the remembrance of thy wrongs. But, alas! thou art not the only victim of the remorseless rum traffic. From many households has it borne away the fair, the good, and all the heart holds precious. Alas, its premature graves disfigure every hill-side and every plain.

When shall this great evil cease? Christians, philanthropists, law-makers, when?

INCIDENT IN A DEPOT.

I WAS pacing the floor, impatiently waiting the arrival of the steamer. The other passengers had come in, till the seats in the "gentlemen's room" were quite filled, when the door again opened and a woman entered. She held in her hands some boxes of blacking, and approaching me, as the person nearest the door, offered them for sale. I had scarcely declined purchasing, when, noticing the woman more closely, I regretted not having favored her. Her face was pale, sad, and careworn. Her dress was neat, yet cheap and scant, and her manner timid in the extreme. It was plain that my refusal had well nigh frightened away her small stock of courage, for she stood irresolute a moment, as if fearing a similar repulse from others to whom she might apply; then, summoning resolution, she passed to the man at my right, and asked, faintly, "Will you buy some blacking, sir?"

He also shook his head. She paused once more with a pained look, then mutely tendered the boxes to each person in the room, going unsuccessfully round the entire circle. The last one accosted was a young sailor, in tarpaulin and blue jacket. He sat leaning over a paper, reading, when she found voice to say, despondently, ". Won't you take a box?"

By this time the attention of all the persons present was fixed on her with deepening interest. The downcast eyes; the alternate pallor and crimson of cheek, and neck, and brow; the slow, hesitating step, now advancing, now stopping, as if powerless to proceed; utterance overcome by emotion, — impressed us that some great trouble or an inexorable emergency had brought her thus before us.

"I don't want your blacking," said the seaman, heartily; "and if I did, 'twould be of no use to me, for I am more than two hundred miles from home; but if you want money," drawing forth a handful of loose change, "you can have it!" At the first movement of his hand pocketward, before his words had interpreted the action, most of the men present, with evident feeling, were doing the same, and, pouring their united contributions into the apron of the astonished woman, she retired, overpowered with gratitude and joy.

As I stepped aboard the boat I thought, how eloquent is silence! No tale of sorrow did this woman present to excite pity. Her mute appeal was understood. And is not many a good cause injured, rather than helped, by the wordiness of its advocates? Are we not often conscious of internal revolt, as we listen to verbose appeals to our sympathies, whether on behalf of private or public charities? We get accustomed to declamation, to argument, and to peroration, but who can resist sincerity, modesty, sensibility, — the condensed, broken, or speechless plea of a full heart?

And then, too, the power of example, — of frank, disinterested, beneficent action, — do we ponder this as we ought? The generous sailor, in his homely sea-garb, led nearly a score of men that day in the work of mercy, and the lowliest and poorest are never so low and poor as to be without the opportunity and means of influencing others by efficiency in well-doing.

MY STEP-MOTHER.

I WAS six years of age when she came to fill the terrible void caused by the death of my mother. I can well remember how we children drew back from the stranger who had come to take her place. There were seven of us; each an idolater at the shrine of our dear mother's memory. The oldest, who possessed a quick, bright intellect, and was somewhat willful withal, quite resented the idea of a second mother. Her strong hostility was contagious, for she was at the head of domestic affairs. Then some sympathizing neighbor would place her hand on my head and say, compassionately, " Poor boy! You'll have a hard time trying to make a mother out of a mother-in-law. She'll never feel toward you as if you were her own child."

Well, one day I was measured for a new suit of clothes. Other articles of toilet to correspond came ere long. Indeed, there seemed to be a general refurnishing throughout house and household. What it all meant I could not conjecture, and no one told me. Then one afternoon there came a universal scrubbing of the faces and hands of the children, and we were all dressed in our best clothes. There was something unusual about to take place. What could it be? Not a meeting, for no such preparation, that is, in kind and spirit, ever preceded those staid religious gatherings often witnessed in our large, old-fashioned parlor. Still, a hush and a gravity pervaded the busy household, imparting a sort of half-and-half aspect, somewhat festive and somewhat solemn. At length the important secret was condescendingly communicated to me.

"Now," said my eldest sister, as she combed my hair back *a la Maffitt*, (for like other sentimentally inclined young ladies of the town, she had been captivated with the Irish preacher's eloquence), "do you behave like a little man this evening, for father's going to be married, and we are all to be at the wedding!"

"Wedding! What do they do there?"

"Why, you little dunce, there'll be a whole parlor full of folks, and the minister will be there and make a speech and pray, and marry father and his bride, and then cake and wine will be passed around to all the company. You'll get a large slice of the best cake you ever ate, and a sip of the wine, and then — why, then you see, you'll have a *step*-mother to train you up in the way you should go. How will you like that?"

Bolt upright, in an exceedingly uncomfortable position, on a stiff, hard chair, scarcely daring to wink, I sat on that eventful night. Several relatives of the bride spoke kindly to me, without, in the least, relaxing my mental and muscular rigidity, till one of them, since known as the most lovable of aunts, brought me a piece of handsomely frosted cake, and a glass of wine, both of which I supposed were mysterious parts of the mysterious marriage rite. Though how eating and drinking helped to give me a new mother I did not comprehend.

"Take it all, dear!" said she, sinking down before me on the carpet, as I diffidently broke off a crumb of the cake. "It's yours, and you have just as good a right to it as any body, if you *are* a little boy."

I obeyed, thinking it a part of the ceremony, gazing the while into her black eyes, that were soft, and limpid, and loving.

Our new mother went home with us that night, for the marriage was at "Aunt Abby's." What a prim set we were indeed! What a constraint was on us, knowing a mother-in-law was installed in the home, to reign over us, her unwilling subjects. Very undemocratic it seemed, certainly, for we hadn't cast a vote nor been consulted even! However, the general awkwardness was relieved by her leaving home on a bridal visit. She was to be gone a fortnight. How glad we were!

How we dreaded her return, gossiping about it, hoping it might be protracted. But she came promptly back to her post, and, spite of my suspicions, I couldn't help a warm glow as she kissed us each, and, unpacking her trunk, gave the presents she had brought us. Her cordial, motherly greeting was a shock to our prejudices, from which they did not at once recover. But objections to the step-mother of a more personal nature were soon discussed.

"To think that your father should marry a *country* woman, farm-born and bred," said one. "She can not have seen any thing of society, and must be coarse and low. And your first mother was a perfect lady!"

"New brooms sweep clean," suggested another, "but look out for black eyes; they are always deceitful!"

Poor, dear woman! little did she know what a burden she was assuming in becoming the wife of a widower with seven children, who had been taught to distrust her noblest actions, and set her authority at defiance. But meagerly could she forecast the toil and anxiety, the heart-griefs and perplexities that were to wait on her footsteps daily; the gloomy hours of sickness and of death; the battlings with pecuniary reverses; the clothing, and feeding, and nurturing of those henceforward to call her mother. But, having put her hand to the plow, she did not turn back from the heavy responsibilities of her lot. With a heroic endurance, a sublime self-forgetfulness, that, a thousand times since assuming manhood's cares have filled me with wonder as I have retraced her history, did she press forward, conquering difficulties, winning triumphs, until, without a peer, she sat enthroned in our love in her beautiful, I had almost said angelic goodness, and costly devotion.

Ah! what would have become of us without *her?* What a marvel of a worker she was! Early and late at her tasks, never lagging, turning off labor with a despatch that few might hope to rival. The sweet breath of the country, its good, honest fare, its healthful scenes, — what would she have done as *our* mother without the firm-toned constitution they had molded. And in her little tripping way, as she almost flew about house, how graceful!

Rarely did she administer chastisement, however richly deserved, for she well knew that officious critics would intermeddle. She referred our misdemeanors to father. Though even then, there were those who intimated before us that she loved to find fault with her step-children.

One day an incident laid bare her heart in some measure to my eyes.

I had been perverse, disrespectful, disobedient. As a punishment, she sent me to bed supperless. I knew the punishment was deserved, but went to my room muttering complaints. At length I fell asleep. How long I remained thus I do not know, but suddenly waking I saw her kneeling at the bedside, her face pale, and her eyes mournfully fixed upon me.

"Oh," said she, gently, "I am so glad you awoke. You lay so still I was almost afraid you were not alive; I was listening to hear if you breathed. Are you well, dear? I came in to see. I know it's hard for you to go without your supper; it was hard for me to punish you, but I *do* want you to be a good boy, that you may grow up a good and useful man!" Then, after a moment's pause, in eager tones, she continued, "Do you really think, dear child, that I love to find fault with you? or that I wronged you to-night in what I said or did?"

Thus did she yearn after me with a mother's solicitude, and humble herself to plead with me after my wanton disobedience. My heart melted, and I said, "I have been a naughty, selfish boy, and you have been too kind to me. I deserved to be punished. I want you to forgive and love me."

How tenderly she imprinted a kiss upon my forehead, and fervently imploring God's blessing, glided from the room.

Hers was a rugged path for the most part, such as one sees running up a mountain side, over roots, and stones, and brambles. From what secret spring did she derive her more than human strength? Where obtain the patience and fortitude that glorified her daily character? Ah! is there more than one fountain-head? Rising before day, while yet the occupants of the house were wrapped in sleep, she would retire to a little room and pour out her soul in fervent prayer. Sometimes the still air of the morning twilight has seemed to my quickened sensibilities to be pervaded and throbbing, as if her very soul, in its fervent pleadings, filled the space around me. Strangely thrilled, I have listened, wondering at the feeling that oppressed me; awe, sadness, self-dissatisfaction, desires for a better life crowding upon the mind, as the plaintive, tremulous voice could just be heard. When she had left communing with her divine Friend, and we met her at the morning meal, no one would fail to be struck with her aspect; serious, serene, trustful — peace, Christ's peace, impressed upon her brow. You would take knowledge of her that she had been with Jesus.

"Ah!" said one, "when she has children of her own then you'll see a difference!"

Well, Lizzie, with her dark, reflective eyes, came. Afterwards plump little Sarah, with her hazel orbs. And was it not a miracle that half-sisters and brothers grew so into unity as to need to be reminded that the full relation was not theirs!

How often I have collected my scattered faculties, as if to master a new thought, when a visitor remarked, "These are your step-sisters, I suppose?"

"Step-sisters!" I would reply. "Oh, yes, I had forgotten it!" quickly to forget it again.

And what a love was hers! What delicate, far-reaching sympathies! what boundless charity! what intuitive perception of other's rights, and ready, persuasive championship of the unappreciated and the wronged. What genial, winning ways towards the young; how self-denyingly benevolent. And as age enfeebled her step and silvered her head, growing younger and younger in her tastes, responding to the innocent jest, delighting in innocent enjoyments, charming every one with her kind words and kind deeds.

"Grandmother is coming!" Henry, the youngest, would exclaim, as he rushed into the house to be first with the good news.

Sure enough. Feebly tripping along,

with a mysterious package, too heavy for her strength, under her arm, she would approach, panting with exertion, her face radiant with affection.

"O mother!" we would say, "you have taken too much pains to see us — the walk is too much for you!"

"Don't say a word!" she would answer, deprecatingly; "I couldn't stay away any longer. I must know how you all do. And here," undoing her bundle, "are some little things I have brought for the children."

Her energetic heart grew in wealth of love marvelously, and her sympathies embraced the world. But specially among her kindred did their quick and active power appear. It was strange to us how soon she became aware of it, if any trouble invaded our ranks.

One night, sudden, evil news, of which none knew but ourselves, kept our little circle sleepless. We lived remote from the maternal roof. Next morning, calling there, mother took me aside and said, "Tell me, my son, if you were unhappy last night. I must know, for I could not sleep — you were on my mind so. It seemed to me that you were in trouble!"

But she's gone. Three weeks ago today, over the wires flew the message: "*Mother is very sick, and can live only a few hours?*"

Then immediately following came the crushing announcement of her death.

But she passed away as she had lived. In usual health she stood by her chair, about to take her seat at the dinner-table, uttering one of her pleasant remarks, when the wing of the death angel touched her;

she fell, speechless, unconscious, and never revived. It was as if the loving Saviour designed her last words should be like her, should represent her, and from the family board her spirit went up to the kindred hearts around the feast-table of heaven.

Dear, noble, sainted mother! how can we bear to see thee no more and hear no more thy words of love! But thou art safe, happy, robed in glory.

www.ingramcontent.com/pod-product-compliance
Lightning Source LLC
Chambersburg PA
CBHW030748230426
43667CB00007B/881